Interdisciplinary
MENTORING IN SCIENCE

T0383361

Interdisciplinary
MENTORING IN SCIENCE
Strategies for Success

OFELIA A. OLIVERO PhD

AMSTERDAM • BOSTON • HEIDELBERG • LONDON
NEW YORK • OXFORD • PARIS • SAN DIEGO
SAN FRANCISCO • SINGAPORE • SYDNEY • TOKYO
Academic Press is an imprint of Elsevier

Academic Press is an imprint of Elsevier
The Boulevard, Langford Lane, Kidlington, Oxford, OX5 1GB, UK
225 Wyman Street, Waltham, MA 02451, USA

Copyright © 2014 Elsevier Inc. All rights reserved

No part of this publication may be reproduced, stored in a retrieval system or transmitted
in any form or by any means electronic, mechanical, photocopying, recording or
otherwise without the prior written permission of the publisher.

Permissions may be sought directly from Elsevier's Science & Technology Rights
Department in Oxford, UK: phone (+44) (0) 1865 843830; fax (+44) (0) 1865 853333;
email: permissions@elsevier.com. Alternatively, visit the Science and Technology Books
website at www.elsevierdirect.com/rights for further information.

Notice
No responsibility is assumed by the publisher for any injury and/or damage to persons or
property as a matter of products liability, negligence or otherwise, or from any use or
operation of any methods, products, instructions or ideas contained in the material
herein. Because of rapid advances in the medical sciences, in particular, independent
verification of diagnoses and drug dosages should be made.

British Library Cataloguing-in-Publication Data
A catalogue record for this book is available from the British Library

Library of Congress Cataloging-in-Publication Data
A catalog record for this book is available from the Library of Congress

ISBN: 978-0-12-415962-4

For information on all Academic Press publications
visit our website at http://store.elsevier.com

Typeset by MPS Limited, Chennai, India
www.adi-mps.com

Working together
to grow libraries in
developing countries

ELSEVIER   Book Aid International

www.elsevier.com • www.bookaid.org

DEDICATION

To Ovidio Núñez,
Mentor of mentors

"Outstanding! Dr. Olivero's interdisciplinary or I-Mentor model is in-step with the growing trend of team and relational approaches to professional life. In addition, she recognizes synchronicity and collective group experience as important elements in the I-Mentoring process."

Richard H. Geer, Author, Star Journey Symbol Method, Walnut Creek, California

"Dr. Olivero provides an approach to interdisciplinary science that is not merely cross-cultural, but multi-dimensionally cross-cultural. Not only does the interdisciplinary mentor in team science have to deal with ethnic diversity, but also the deep, under-appreciated challenges of science-culture diversity. Dr. Olivero provides special emphasis on these issues to coach the would-be mentor to develop the needed sensitivity to handle the complex human interactions of today's science research team."

Thomas Meylan, PhD, retired astrophysicist

"Dr. Olivero's book on mentoring will be a valuable resource for potential mentors as well as for mentees. Mentorship is the cornerstone of the young scientist's education...I believe that this book will be particularly illuminating to independent researchers who are deeply immersed in cutting edge, highly specialized research. Those entrenched in the principles of classic mentoring may miss the opportunity to influence the young students in the principles of a new era of scientific investigation."

Félix Fernández-Madrid, MD, PhD, FACP, Professor of Internal Medicine, Wayne State University, Detroit, Michigan

CONTENTS

ACKNOWLEDGMENTS

To my family, because they believed in me and helped me advance.

To all my mentees, who are an essential part of the mentor I am today.

To my mentors, the role models who imparted the many messages that are now multiplied through the new generation.

To Andy and Kristine, who made the publishing process enjoyable by being extremely supportive.

To all of you who made this possible. Thanks for your support and encouragement.

To all the mentors who, day after day, change people's lives without asking anything in return.

BIOGRAPHY

The author was born and educated in Argentina. She came to the US to train as a cancer researcher, and is now a Senior Staff Scientist at a large biomedical research facility in Bethesda, Maryland. Motivated by the educational gap and the lack of minority groups in science, she took every opportunity to attract minorities to her laboratory to generate a more diverse environment. She has trained numerous students and empowered them to believe in themselves and pursue careers in science. Once she realized that there was virtually no information on the topic of mentoring in the sciences, she took the initiative to write this book. She mentions that the book is the result of her experiences as a mentee, her discussions with peers in Latin America, her life as a mentor, and the need to produce a change in mental outlook in some circles. Motivated by the emerging field of the Science of Team Science, she realized that the moment for new mentoring had arrived, and that the new generations needed to have training and built-in awareness of the science of the future. She has therefore written this book in the hope of helping mentors and mentees to engage in collaborative science and to generate a new environment able to welcome creativity and blend the multiple talents of a diverse scientific community. The "kaleidoscope effect" summarizes these ideas in a new concept that is easy to explain and familiar to everyone, regardless of cultural background. Dr Olivero is the mother of three daughters and lives in Maryland with her husband.

Photo courtesy of Carol Jones.

FOREWORD

Despite increased attention to the importance of mentoring in advancing interdisciplinary science, the practice remains uneven. As a result, both mentors and mentees are often uncertain about the definition of mentoring, the process, and the unique requirements of interdisciplinary mentoring in particular. Ofelia Olivero answers many of their questions while offering an array of examples, lessons from practice, insights from interviews, and the I-Mentoring program model. The book's interrogative approach, complete with exercises, makes it simultaneously a self-directed reading and a group-training resource. It is a deeply personal book, informed by Olivero's own experience and crafted as an invitation for readers to chart autobiographical journeys of their own.

The customary feedback relationship between individuals that characterizes mentoring is made complex when working across disciplinary and professional boundaries. A single mentor may not be knowledgeable about multiple areas of expertise, requiring the cooperation of multiple mentors. In either case, individual and community both benefit from the forging of new relationships based on mutuality. Diversities of status, gender, race, and ethnicity further underscore the importance of negotiating difference while asserting the value of self-definition.

The emergence of Science of Team Science as a recognized platform for boundary-crossing collaborative research only underscores the urgency of cultivating capacity for addressing complex problems and questions in the next generation of researchers and educators. Doing so will require not only flexible organizational structures and dynamic work cultures. It also requires fostering skills of communication, cooperation, collaboration, consensus, and commitment across disciplines, professions, ranks, and institutions. Couched in caveats and coached by guidelines, *Interdisciplinary Mentoring in Science* charts an interdisciplinary perspective on achieving these goals.

Julie Thompson Klein
Faculty Fellow for Interdisciplinary
Development in the Division of Research
and Professor of Humanities in the English
Department, Wayne State University
Detroit, MI, USA

CHAPTER 1

Mentoring Definition—The Mentor Within

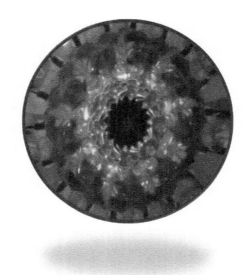

DEFINITION OF MENTORING

Mentoring is a process of continuous and dynamic feedback between two individuals to establish a relationship through which one person shares knowledge, skills, information, and perspective to foster the personal and professional growth of the other.

THE MENTOR WITHIN

It would be of little value to supply a list of the ideal qualities required for mentoring. The aspiring mentor is likely to be so discouraged by the sheer number of characteristics required that

Interdisciplinary Mentoring in Science
DOI: http://dx.doi.org/10.1016/B978-0-12-415962-4.00001-1
© 2014 Elsevier Inc.
All rights reserved.

they either give up or close themselves to learning more about the subject.

Instead, I prefer to facilitate the empowering of my readers, enabling them to perform a deep self-assessment, to connect with themselves and find their real wishes and motivations with regard to mentoring.

Although is not easy to motivate scientists to focus on internal topics, I have found that many are willing to participate and look inside themselves. Firstly, if they signed up to be part of a mentoring effort (rather than a mandatory training demanded to fulfill academic obligations), or if they acquired this book or find themselves reading it for some other reason, then their motivation is there. Secondly, if they are part of a mentoring forum with the same common goal, to be better at something, to learn, to understand better, the motivation is also there. They want to be part of the effort, and all of them share a common interest. That is already very valuable. If someone has signed up to attend a class of this type, even more if they had to pay to attend, they will be open and receptive. Provided that that is the case, a motivational speech, rather than a laundry list of qualities, should be offered.

> *The mentor within has much more value than the laundry list in becoming a good mentor.*
>
> *The mentor within is the real energy that individuals put to work once discovered. The gesture, the attitude, the good feeling of empowering others, of facilitating them to grow, starts developing and presents as a natural force within. Once discovered, the force reshapes itself and becomes clearer, almost as an instinct.*

The real exercise, to find the mentor within, combines the introspection of the individual looking to become a mentor with facilitation through a slow process guided by a coach. This approach, interestingly, works for those who have experienced good mentoring in their lives, as well as for those who cannot identify a real mentor in their careers.

Since the power of gratitude goes beyond past experiences, the event of recreating the feeling inside oneself invigorates the quality of mentoring inside us. Reviving that energy is the clue, it is the secret to finding the mentor within.

Being more connected to ourselves helps to facilitate the connection to others, improves perceptions about others, and aids in identification of the talents of the mentee. This is one of the most important skills of a mentor, the ability to identify skills and qualities in the people that they are mentoring.

EXERCISE

In this book, you will find exercises that will guide you to learn the art of mentoring. Those will also be useful to you when trying to implement your own mentoring program.

For this exercise, I suggest that you find a quiet place that you feel comfortable in. It could be your garden, your favorite chair, your bed; you can also read it now, and practice it while working out, or jogging. The clue is to have a "my time" time.

Try to have a glass of water next to you and also some nice music if you can, not distracting, but reflective. Think about this when you conduct this experience for others. It is critical that you experience it yourself first to appreciate the value of it and be able to facilitate it for others.

Once you collect yourself and feel quiet and convinced that the next few minutes can be devoted to this activity exclusively, try to remember an episode in which you experienced gratitude towards someone. Try to refresh that episode in which you were treated with genuine kindness, without expecting anything in return.

Think about it, recall it to yourself, remember details, places, phrases, gestures, remember as much as you can. If necessary, start over again from the beginning of the story to recreate the feeling. How did you feel? Can you recapture that sensation now? Can you experience the satisfaction that you experienced then? Take a deep breath, close your eyes and stay with the feeling. Stay with the reaction, the story now is not the focus. The focus is yourself, what is going through you now. Try to identify the feeling with a name, a nickname, if needed. Open your eyes when you are ready, but do not let go of the feeling.

Drink your water, breathe deeply, feel good. Gratitude is a great feeling. The reason why I chose to center the first exercise around gratitude is because I consider it critical in the search for the mentor within.

Mentoring is in most cases the transference of gratitude. It is well known that most of us like to transfer experience to our mentees. We have been there, done that, and like to forewarn others by telling them in advance what is there for them. It is also well known that most of the time that does not work, and experience cannot be transferred. Knowledge is something else that a mentor would like to transfer to share with their mentees; however, in many cases, knowledge is something the mentees will acquire in their own academic careers.

Gratitude, however, is one quality that can be transferred.

Let's go back to your episode, the one described at the beginning of this exercise. When you were treated with kindness, when the feeling of gratitude emerged from you and developed, what was the immediate reaction that filled your mind? Did you not feel an immediate need to return the favor? Did you not experience the need to treat somebody else with kindness to return the attitude? Gratitude is something that moves us so deeply that it makes us givers, after being receivers.

That is why I consider that developing the feeling of gratitude (which not everyone is able to recognize), being able to identify the feeling, is so relevant to being able to find the mentor within.

When the mentor offers genuine advice, when they care, when the time and the attention devoted to the mentee are truly honest, the mentee experiences that feeling you experienced a long time ago—"gratitude." Imagine a world where everybody feels that way towards each other. That is too much, I know. Well, imagine a world where you can make a difference to others, where you can facilitate other people's lives, where you can produce change, positive change, where the feeling of gratitude will be experienced by others thanks to your actions, your thoughts, your acts. Even more, imagine that the person you touched in that positive way is going to return that, to give it back to others, who in turn ... you get the picture.

But as I mentioned before not everybody is able to recognize kindness or to express gratitude. Some people simply feel in debt to others who helped them or did something for them. Even more, they reciprocate because they feel obliged to do so. That is not what I mean by gratitude. Gratitude is much more than reciprocity. Some people feel entitled to others' actions, others believe they deserved whatever someone else did for them. There are many of those around us. I feel sorry for them, and I wish they could all experience the feeling that we discussed previously, realizing that the actions of others toward us do not even need to be big things for us to feel good about them and to experience gratitude to them and others.

I would like to cite an example here of those who have difficulties in either perceiving or expressing gratitude. I am going to paraphrase my friend Rose, who has been kind enough to let me use her name and all her experiences in order to help others. I need to express gratitude towards her!

Rose's daughter Margaret had the great opportunity to obtain an internship in a prestigious university. She learned a lot during the three summer months that she spent among scientists, gels, and fruit flies. At the end of her internship, Rose asked Margaret: "Today is your last day with them, what are you going to take to the laboratory to show gratitude, to express appreciation for everything they did for you?" Margaret did not seem to understand. She felt entitled, she probably thought that they had to do whatever they did for her, and she did not have to recognize anybody in any special manner. The question posed by Margaret rapidly grew into an argument that ended on an ugly note. Rose was upset because of her daughter's selfishness, and was also concerned that she was not capable of recognizing kindness and experiencing gratitude. One entire year passed and the topic was not mentioned again. The following summer, Margaret was able to secure another internship, this time in a different laboratory in the same institution. Being smart and knowing that it was better to keep quiet, Rose did not ask Margaret this time about her last day and what she would do for the people who had helped her. To Rose's surprise Margaret cooked cupcakes for everybody, decorated them carefully and wrote thank you cards individually to more than 10 people. That was it. It took a long time for Margaret to understand and experience it, but I am sure, as much as Rose is, that Margaret is a much better person now and has a much better life. In addition, because she expressed gratitude to all those individuals, they in turn may do the same for others. Gratitude, according to Robert Emmons in his book *Thanks*, inspires us to open our hearts more widely to others. In his book, he encourages readers to practice 'grateful thinking' as a way to increase good sleep, have more energy and improve overall wellbeing. His contributions are part of the positive psychology movement also embraced by Dr. Barbara Frederickson, who wrote the book

Positivity, in which she illustrated with abundant scientific data, the importance of positive thinking, and even more so, of positive feeling. Dr. Frederickson shows how new discoveries support the notion that this new state of mind can improve relationships and health, and may even help to alleviate depression.

One of my students, Juan Fernandez, was the first in his family of immigrants to attend college. He expressed gratitude by saying this:

> *Our parents came to work to this country to clean houses for us to be able to attend college and get an education. We have a moral obligation to make a change.*

WHAT THE EXPERTS HAVE TO SAY

Interview with Dr. Linda Kupfer, Office of Global AIDS Coordinator (OGAC) President's Emergency Plan for AIDS Relief (PEPFAR) Department of State.

What is Mentoring?

Question 1. Would you mind telling us about your background?
I have a PhD in pharmacology, 10 years at the National Institutes for Health (NIH) in the Office of Policy, Planning, and Evaluation in Global Health.

Question 2. What areas are you covering in the global health arena? Could you specify?
I would say my background is in monitoring and evaluation as well as capacity building. Additionally I have an interest in implementation research.

Question 3. What type of work do you do, and for how long have you being doing it?

I was an American Association for the Advancement of Sciences (AAAS) fellow at the State Department, and I also worked at the office of International Sciences at NOAA (National Oceanic and Atmospheric Administration). For a time, I worked in my actual field at NOAA as a Program Officer, in marine biotechnology and pharmaceuticals from the sea. I was managing a small program called the Sea Grant in marine biotechnology. I have been working in the government for 26 years.

Question 4. You have been chosen to respond to questions related to the definition of mentoring. Is that a topic you feel confident about covering?

Sure. I think that because I have had a variety of positions, some of which did not fit the traditional career path, I am able to talk to people who want to change careers, going from science to policy, or going into global health from another field of science. Those are the individuals that contact me most of the time, the ones that are doing research and want to move to global health careers. The fact that I started in the basic sciences and moved to policy and then global health makes me something of a role model for those that are considering that type of change.

Question 5. What would be your advice to people who are trying to change fields?

To be successful in this transition I always advise my mentees to:

1. Acquire knowledge in the new field to which they want to transition. For that reason, I started a course at NIH on

global health. I suggest that trainees obtain good background knowledge before interviewing for a new position. This is critical and helps not to waste everyone's time.

2. Developing a project with the mentee is very useful. I have started a program at OGAC to develop mentoring programs in academic institutions in sub-Saharan Africa (SSA). In developing countries, the highest degree obtained is usually a Master's degree. A PhD degree or postdoctoral experience, which is very common here, is still virtually unknown in SSA. The programs that are being developed in universities in SSA revolve around projects. This encourages the mentor and mentee to work together, and to obtain a tangible result after collaboration. The NIH course in global health was developed by one of my mentees.

Question 6. For a person who chose the non-classical track, would you concede that a Master's degree or a PhD is not the only track?

I would say that that is true, but one has to be careful. Today there are many people with BAs. To distinguish yourself, especially in the sciences, you may need a masters or a PhD. It really depends on the work you want to do. For global health, one of the most important things to have is experience in a developing country. You may get this through a fellowship, internship or other work experience.

Question 7. Do you think there are specific challenges in the topic of mentoring that need to be addressed?

I do. I think that there is a lack of curriculum for mentoring, and a lack of standards for being a mentor.

Question 8. So we mentor based on our instincts, but the concept of one size fits all does not necessarily apply, is that correct?

Exactly. I think that there are best practices that could be studied and shared to help teach people about mentoring. I also think that people should be screened prior to allowing them to be a mentor.

Question 9. You have lived in two different worlds, both the laboratory bench and administration. I am sure that you have witnessed the prevalence of mentoring in the latter area. Why do you think the practice is not so much appreciated in the scientific arena?

I do not think the practice is as prevalent as you think it is in administration. The concept of mentoring has to be valued by the senior level administrators for it to be successfully implemented. For example, in many organizations, mentoring is not recognized as a metric for career promotion. In that case, the incentive to mentor is greatly decreased. Mentoring needs to be an organizational value to be successful and sustainable within the organization.

Question 10. Do you have any strategy when it comes to mentoring to be particularly effective?

I try to make sure that my door is always open and that I have regular meetings with the mentee. I always like to have a joint project with the mentee, something we develop together. I also like a mentor—mentee contract, so that there is agreement and articulation on what is expected from each party.

Question 11. What about the role of the supervisor and the mentor when they overlap?

I do not think your supervisor should be your mentor. As a mentee, you have to talk about limitations, fears and weaknesses, things that you might not want your supervisor to be aware of. A supervisor could be a partial mentor, but someone else should be the main mentor.

Question 12. Is there any change in the traditional practice of mentoring that you would envision to improve the practice in the setting of modern mentoring?

One of the women who has a mentoring program in South Africa has an interesting approach. She employs a panel of mentors for the mentees in the program, because they do not have enough individuals to do one-on-one mentoring. The mentoring group therefore comprises committed faculty members. It helps that the group is multidisciplinary in nature, although this was not the original reason why it was set up. It is quite compelling. They also put together Journal Clubs, to speak about the different disciplines and different projects. The value of such a group became obvious once it had been implemented.

Question 13. Could you give some specific advice for mentors?

"Do it," if you want to. If you have never been a mentor and are unsure of your talent in this area, you can start with a program that provides books, curriculum and agreements to train and empower the mentor.

Question 14. Could you provide some words of wisdom for the mentees?

It is up to the mentee to put effort into finding a good mentor. Interview the mentor first to see if they are a good fit for you. Mentees must be active participants in the mentor—mentee relationship.

Question 15. Anything else you would like to add?

I do not think so. I appreciate you choosing me for this interview.

CHAPTER NOTES AND OBSERVATIONS

In this section, you are welcome to write your notes. You could use the following system, provided that you have some time to dedicate to it.

First, just write, do not worry about processing. Just write the first thing that comes to your mind. Use this space to do it. Extend the writing as much as you want or simply write one sentence, or even perhaps just one word. We will call that section *Brainstorming*.

In the second section, you are invited to reflect. The section will be your space to elaborate more about your brainstorming to organize the thoughts and make sense of them. That second section will be called *Reflection*. Although you can work on that section immediately after you have finished your brainstorming, it is advisable to come back to it later, the next day or even a week or two after the brainstorming took place. Unlike the first section, this second one will call for a more organized style of writing, where the brainstorming ideas crystallize to form concepts that you own, that you generated from yourself. Note that those concepts could align with the reading, or differ from it. It does not matter. Those are the concepts you generated through your own elaboration.

Finally, you can summarize, perhaps with the help of bullet points or short sentences, the most outstanding ideas or concepts from the topic. That section, typically shorter than the former ones will be named *Conclusion*.

I invite you to start with this chapter.

Brainstorming

_____

_____

_____

_____

_____

_____

_____

Reflection

_____

_____

_____

_____

_____

_____

_____

Conclusion

_____

_____

CHAPTER 2

What Mentoring Is Not

A VERTICAL RELATIONSHIP

A vertical relationship implies hierarchy, steps and differences.

Mentoring, on the other hand, is a relationship of mutual respect, regardless of the professional position of the individuals involved.

It is not surprising to discover that most people who are asked to think about a mentor or imagine a mentor direct their minds towards an old person who looks at them from above. Although that concept has evolved, the stimulation of our brains remains fixed on that archaic vision of the concept.

Because traditionally in academia students are matched to mentors who are on a higher step on their careers, it is not

Interdisciplinary Mentoring in Science
DOI: http://dx.doi.org/10.1016/B978-0-12-415962-4.00002-3
© 2014 Elsevier Inc.
All rights reserved.

surprising that the idea of hierarchy is still prevalent in the majority of individuals.

On the other hand, the concept of mentoring as a relationship of mutual respect, regardless of the position of the individuals involved, clearly indicates a different approach. Perhaps some examples will be useful to illustrate this point. In his work *Intelligent Mentoring*, Murrellby describes examples of a famous US company in which mentoring took place by creating value through people, knowledge, and relationships. The concept seems simple; however, it surprised more than one employee. One of the examples cited in the book refers to an unexpected situation encountered by the mentee. He happened to be a long-serving member of the company, those regarded as possessing the organizational memory, and frequently consulted as a reference point and information source. This person was working late once and could not solve an issue with his computer. It was very important to move forward this project that kept him working until midnight. Looking for help, he found only one person whom he barely knew, since that person was quite new, young, and probably not one of the "company men," with his unconventional hours and non-traditional attire. However, he was a computer literate individual, with knowledge exceeding that of older, more traditional employees. Moved by the emergency, the needy employee asked the younger one to help him. Not only was the problem solved, but some teaching was also involved and some skills were transferred. That was the beginning of a new relationship that transcended the episode and was built from an immediate need, but was transformed into mutual respect by the parties involved.

A very rudimentary analysis of the situation above described suggests that failure to establish fruitful work relationships generally arises from certain assumptions. Assumptions that because one has been in a company for a long time, no new knowledge is needed, or that new non-traditional young employees have nothing to teach but a lot to learn, are misconceptions. They fuel the idea that mentoring goes from old to young or from experienced to novice; this is not always the case.

Although it may be true that most mentoring goes from senior to junior partner, emphasis should be placed on welcoming and embracing the concept of horizontal, rather than vertical, mentoring, in the workplace, academia, or any other setting that requires mentoring.

Consider the examples frequently seen in academia, where the more traditional professors benefit from the new technology brought by savvy individuals who join their laboratories, or teaching rooms. Similarly, the plethora of information abundantly disseminated in the cyberspace is more easily navigated by the younger generations than the old ones. Access to technology, is second nature for those who were born with a computer in their nursery, rather than a radio.

Transferring knowledge, skills, or expertise from junior to senior workers generates a great sense of respect in both directions, not only for those receiving the information, but also, for those giving it. There is also great respect for those that are in senior positions, but have the modesty to recognize their limitations in some areas and are eager to learn new concepts, ideas and skills. Mentoring in both directions does not diminish hierarchies, but rather empowers both individuals to trust each other, to help each other and to work in a balanced environment where there is no giver or receiver as such, but two individuals growing together, by learning from each other.

In order to make this process efficient, changes in mentality, and attitude are required. All parties need to embrace a different kind of working relationship. In the case of the mentor, understanding that receiving advice or transferring of skills, or understanding a new point of view from a junior person, is a valid dimension that should be embraced when necessary. The junior individual should be able to perceive the attitude of a senior employee, perhaps his/her supervisor, not as a loss of authority, or a change in the established hierarchy, but rather a learning approach that should be celebrated and accepted. A third change in the workforce may be experienced by work colleagues in general, who should perceive this new type of interaction as a genuine mentor—mentee relationship that could be the beginning of a new cultural change in the organization, an example of future fruitful relationships. Mentor and mentee should work together in the understanding that the new dynamic is not just limited to the learning of a particular skill, but should continue as a more mature and long-term relationship.

Mutual respect is the base of this new relationship that will provide a new path to navigate and to grow personally and professionally. Emily Wadsworth, in her book *Giving Much/Gaining More*, characterizes trust as the ability to believe in the honesty, responsibility, integrity, loyalty and dependability of the other person. I can imagine many instances where this situation seems to be impossible and unimaginable by many, and that this new vision of mutual benefit may seem like a fantasy. However, a couple of real life examples will help illustrate the real possibility of this concept.

A mentor who is not a supervisor would have much less difficulty in establishing a horizontal relationship rather than a vertical one. Many times, once a dialog is established and two individuals are communicating deeply, the barriers, the obstacles, and the hierarchies disappear. This is because the channel established between these two parties is based on trust. It does not matter how many steps ahead in the company or in the department the person is. At that moment, there is a primary element driving the relationship: trust. Wadsworth reflects on her book about the importance of trusting yourself first. Once you achieve that step, through self-exploration and deep inquiry, you can be trusted and you can trust others. She mentions the example of one of the members of her mentoring group at Perdue. She was an excellent student and accomplished young woman. Once she missed a meeting and did not inform Dr. Wadsworth about it; she was subsequently told the reasons why that would be a challenge to the trust that people had placed in her. It is a simple example, but it taught her to reflect on the expectations of others, based on the trust they deposited on us. Think about your colleagues, and how much they trust that you will be there every day, or that you will teach the class, or run an experiment or give a talk. You will understand that trust is in the smallest things, in attitudes, in words spoken and unspoken, in thoughts, in looks, in every minute of a conversation. Mentors trust their mentees, they have faith in them and in their careers, they believe in them and empower them to do well, to stretch themselves to the limit. On the other hand, mentees trust their mentors because they are the ones in whom they can confide, and who have the knowledge and wisdom to guide them.

A SUPERVISION RELATIONSHIP

A relationship that involves supervision has been pre-established and does not necessarily lead to the personal growth of the individual. The role of mentor could overlap with that of a supervisor, but is not necessarily the ideal situation.

Mentoring is a relationship based on agreement between two individuals, where both of them can benefit and grow.

A traditional mentor—mentee relationship often calls for a supervisor and a supervised type of association. Pre-established relationships most commonly imply that the supervisor will fulfill the role of mentor satisfactorily. Often the words mentor and supervisor are employed interchangeably. Although supervisors can be good mentors, the roles are different. Supervisors often have an interest in the success of their junior and in some cases their careers may depend upon it. This is clearly illustrated by situations in academia, where articles, publications or grants depend in many cases on the work of post-doctoral fellows. There are several instances where the interests of one collide with the interests of the other. It is not unheard of that sometimes the pressures on the supervisor may become transferred to the individuals below them. The Hersey and Blanchard model, which uses situational and leadership theory, proposes a sequence of leadership styles through the evolution of the group being led. For the authors, there is no preferential style of leadership but rather effective task-relevant leadership. The most successful leaders are those who adapt their leadership style to the capacity to set high but attainable goals, willingness and ability to take responsibility for the task, and relevant education and/or experience of an individual or a group for the task. The stages of this process have been explained in detail by Hersey and Blanchard (1977). The understanding of this model will become critical later on in this book, in reference to mentoring in interdisciplinary sciences. Although directed toward a leadership setting, the model could be adapted to the mentoring process.

It is common and widely accepted that at the beginning of the training period of a new student or post-doctoral fellow, the supervisor acts as a mentor and provides guidance, training and close supervision of the trainee. Many successful working relationships have been based on this dynamic. Later on, the trainee gains confidence and acquires independence at a time that usually coincides with a new phase of his or her career and with the search for new horizons. Often this is a critical period during which the supervision and mentor roles diverge. Interested in the production of his/her laboratory, program, or office, the supervisor's interests remain the same as before; however, the trainee's interests start veering towards the future of his or her career. It is at this point that the presence of a mentor is vital. Following the Hersey and Blanchard model, the supervision association at this stage of the relationship should be replaced by a more independent connection. Rarely in a scientific setting, does this situation take place. Supervisors often continue to consider their post-doctoral fellows as supervised individuals who are closely connected with the duties, needs of the program, and demands of the supervisor's careers. Here is where the supervisor role and the mentor role collide, and as a consequence the relationship between mentor and mentee starts to unravel, interests diverge, and frustration arises.

Ideally, then the supervisor and the mentor should be two different individuals. The mentor should be an independent figure, not one who has a vested interest in the permanence of the person in the office or laboratory, whose productivity directly affects the productivity of the supervisor. Rather, the mentor should be completely focused on the individual whom they are advising, in their career, interests, skills, passions and future.

Alternatively, the mentee could work in a close relationship with the supervisor, who fulfills the role of a mentor at the beginning of the trainee's career, since most probably their interests are similar at that point. However, the mentee should be able to establish an independent relationship with a mentor that will last longer than their postdoctoral experience and will guide them in their future scientific career. In some situations, however, the supervisor could feel intimidated or challenged by the presence of a mentor. Except in those cases in which mentors are established by the program, company or academic unit, the fact that the trainee looks for advice outside could generate uneasiness in the mind of the supervisor. This situation needs to be clarified very early in the process.

AN UNEVEN RELATIONSHIP

An uneven relationship implies that the benefit of the relationship goes in one direction, where only one of the members gets the gain. One of the members is passive and expects to receive without control over the decisions.

Mentoring is a relationship of equity where both members participate in a similar fashion, giving and receiving equally.

This is perhaps the most difficult aspect of mentoring to convey. As mentoring is often seen as a vertical relationship, it can be difficult to transform it into a horizontal one. However, please bear with me while I try to demonstrate to you some of the benefits of the relationship for the mentor.

Development of a Human Relation

Plainly said, the fact that the mentor—mentee relationship is a human connection is often overlooked. For many, mentoring is simply an obligation imposed by others, and a job description item that has to be fulfilled to be promoted. For those who chose to be mentors, though, the establishment of a human relationship encompasses all the related benefits. In many instances, mentors are regarded with respect and trust, and the mentor is considered a counselor, with whom many personal matters may be shared. There are many benefits to starting a human relationship, as indicated by Goleman and others.

Improvement of Managerial/Supervisory/Leadership Skills

Establishing this type of human relationship provides a good opportunity to execute many of the skills needed for leadership positions. Giving feedback is one of them. Since giving feedback is one of the most difficult skills to conquer, only overcome by the exercise of receiving feedback, mentoring helps the mentor to polish this skill, by identifying the recipient's abilities and adapting the message to them. A mentor should be able to recognize and identify characteristics of the mentee that would guide the way in which the message is transmitted, so that the effect is positive and empowers the recipient. Feedback is probably the most important element in the relationship, and is also the one most clearly attached to trust. The mentee listens to the feedback the mentor has to offer, trusting the messenger, believing that their best interests are being represented, and also incorporating the changes suggested. It is therefore very important that feedback is given constructively, without ambiguity and in the best possible style. The art of giving feedback should be mastered and adapted to each individual situation. Hence, having a mentee brings a great opportunity to improve that skill that will be applied to multiple working situations.

Network Expansion

Networking capabilities are intensified by the new connections established via the mentee. The exposure to new networks that results from sharing the contacts of the mentee, brings a vast array of possibilities for the mentor. More and more, the advantages of networking are being brought to the attention of those looking for jobs, trying to navigate a new organization, looking for career transition, collaborations, promotions, and growing potential. Richard Nelson Bolles reveals the impact of networking in finding jobs on his book What color is your parachute? He characterizes networks as tribes, and indicates that internet social media allow participants to be part of other tribes, in this way accessing other people's networks, not just their own.

Technology Updates

Often, the mentee brings wide knowledge in the field of technology. Learning from them and having the chance to establish a new dynamic is an added benefit to the mentor—mentee relationship. Many people are not knowledgeable about new technology or computers. Moreover, technology is evolving at such a fast pace that it can be difficult to keep up. For those who were born in the computer age, it is easy to adapt to change and to encounter routes to reach new aspects of technology. There is a potential advantage here for the mentor, since having a person able to understand and transfer knowledge to others is an amazing asset and a way to bridge communication and to make it more solid. It is a means also to increase trust, when knowledge does not come only in one direction but in both. The mentor should remember to acknowledge the new information acquired, thanks to the time and dedication invested by the mentee. Again, recognition and gratitude should be two elements present in this equation.

AN IMPOSED RELATIONSHIP

An imposed relationship is not necessarily the result of a mutual agreement. It usually does not follow the codes or guidelines that are characteristics of relationships that arise from active selection.

Mentoring is a spontaneous relationship based on mutual respect, and implies the establishment of goals to be reached together.

As with many human relationships, people are often presented with choices from which they can select the best option. Friendship, for instance is one of those relationships in which imposition usually does not appear to work. Imposed friendship would be very difficult to accomplish, since often we do not know why we choose the friends we have. In addition, establishing what type of friend will fit well with person A is a very ambitious task, since not all the friends and/or acquaintances of person A look the same, think alike, share the same values, or follow the same paths. Choosing a mentor who may click well with a mentee is as difficult as choosing a friend for person A.

Mentoring programs usually establish what is called a "match," where they associate individuals who may share similar professions, careers or fields. Although desirable, these are not the only reasons or conditions for two individuals to be together. That is why the search for a mentor should be an activity that is initiated by the mentee. An active search and a sense of ownership is part of the entire process of looking for—and finding—the right mentor.

> *Before looking for a mentor, start with a very deep self-reflection exercise. Individuals looking to find a mentor need to look deeply into their selves and reflect on who they are, what they want and the values they hold.*

Additionally, they should have a clear understanding of the values that they want the mentor to share with them. Some values are critical and need to be shared, but others could be different and still permit a valid and successful relationship.

Mentors imposed by a mentoring program or by a school system initiative, or to help individuals in a new setting, classroom or in a new job, can function when both parties agree to work together independently of how they are paired. This may be seen as a limited relationship that is intended to last until the purpose of the relationship is achieved. Then the bond can disappear, and the individuals can part. Such a situation can be successful, and free of frustrations if the limited duration is established *a priori*. Some support groups are often called mentoring groups, and involve people who share a common goal. One example is the successful mentoring group for undergraduate and graduate female students established in 1991 by Dr. Emily Wadsworth in the School of Engineering at Perdue University. The goal of that group was to support women enrolled in the Engineering Program and empower them to the point that they would be successful engineers and would land competitive jobs in a market dominated by men. A diverse group attended the monthly meetings, although the common denominators were gender, profession, and goals. Values could be different, but since the goals and limits of the group were pre-established, the effort was worthwhile and there were positive outcomes for most of the participants.

> *A clear distinction exists when the mentee looks for a mentor who is expected to establish a long-lasting relationship. The search for such a life companion starts with true self-revelation.*

There are unspoken codes in any relationship that operate to determine the beginning of the relationship and its progression.

The future of the relationship depends on how much we bring to it, how much we get in return and how we value, trust, and respect the other person.

A RELATIONSHIP BASED ON "PERSONAL AGENDAS"

A relationship based on personal revenue suggests lack of balance and favoritism towards one of the two members.

Mentoring is a disinterested relationship. The success is measured by the professional and personal growth of both parties.

People who engage in positive and successful relationships usually exercise mutual trust and respect. That is the case for the mentor—mentee relationship as well. The codes mentioned above are unspoken, but both parties understand that they are there for each other and will exercise respect in all actions taken, or advice provided. Generally, but not always, the mentor occupies a more senior position than the mentee. The mentee prefers to relate to a mature person and establishes relationships with individuals who have already navigated the organization they belong to, and taken the paths that the mentee also wishes to follow. Although that is clearly acceptable, there are instances in which the mentee may look to obtain benefits from the mentor's connections, or the possibility to reach out to people who would not be available to the mentee otherwise. That lack of respect is tremendously deleterious for the relationship and for the future of both members. Sooner or later, the objectives of the mentee will become obvious and the frustration of the mentor will determine the cessation of the relationship. Alternatively, the mentor may distance from the mentee. If the mentee is looking to achieve those goals, meeting relevant people, or well connected individuals, that intention should be made clear through discussions with the mentor. There is nothing more despicable than hidden agendas, and in the mentor—mentee relationship, it is completely unacceptable.

By the same token, mentors may also have hidden agendas. In some instances, individuals need to develop mentoring activities to enhance their performance reviews, or to obtain promotions, or special recognitions or awards. In this situation, the only interest of the mentor—their hidden agenda—is to obtain a mentee to add to their resume. In either case, the hidden agenda is not likely to prove useful, and the value of that relationship will be close to zero.

A RELATIONSHIP WITH TIME CONSTRAINTS

A relationship limited by an artificial time frame does not predispose to the success of the goals pre-established by both parties. Mentoring is a relationship without time limitations. Its extent transcends the initial objective.

In academia, mentoring relationships are typically limited by the length of the mentee's stay at the University. Started as a mere counseling exercise the mentor—mentee relationship is established as a guidance process, with a goal. In general, such a relationship is conceived as a professional association. However, as mentioned previously, mentoring transcends the pre-established limits of a relationship and goes beyond a calendar, or a deadline. Perhaps the formal role of mentor ends with the dissertation, or graduation of a mentee or the culmination of a special project or assignment. However, the continuation of the affiliation is highly desirable. Here is where both mentor and mentee should nurture their indestructible bond and try to sustain it. They should not believe that the end of an academic step means the disintegration of their union. Most probably, meetings will take place more sporadically, their times will be harder to arrange, and the geographical location will interfere with chances to meet face to face. However, those who have cultivated a real mentoring relationship will feel the urge to continue. The gratitude felt during the times of interaction will make the relationship durable even with new divergent situations in place. There is no obstacle for two individuals who need to exchange thoughts, talks, or just have an informal chat that will reunite them.

In many instances, "mentoring after the mentoring" is much more relaxed, with no deadlines to fulfill or the rush of a publication to be produced. After the common goal has been achieved, both mentor and mentee can start dedicating their time and interactions to the real personal growth of the individual. It is probable that the mentee is starting a new life, as a graduate, for instance, in a new city, with no many acquaintances, and outside their comfort zone. The mentor role in this case would be orienting the individual, and giving them support, guidance or just sharing experience.

In the research field, a mentoring should not end with the departure of a postdoc. Most probably, the departing individual is looking for their next postdoctoral appointment, or is starting a new job. The mentoring role covers this phase as well, when the novel setting demands a lot of attention and is very stressful.

Once the mentee is settled into their new job and the new directions are mastered, the mentoring effort should still remain alive. The common events that a new life encompasses will present the mentee with many circumstances that deserve discussion. At this point, there is an evolution of the type of exchanges between mentor and mentee. There is a more balanced relationship where there is active listening from both parties, as well as conversation that gravitates more around life issues than professional issues. The mentor receives a lot of information that is new to them, and starts being the passive member rather than the active one. Learning becomes incorporated into the relationship in a different fashion now, where the mentor becomes the recipient, accepting everything that the union provides. Far from being the one who gives advice, now the mentor learns and grows by participating in a relationship in which their role was previously quite different. Those who are open to learning from others will enjoy this stage of the mentoring process, by discovering new horizons through their mentee's life experiences.

WHAT THE EXPERTS HAVE TO SAY

Interview with Dr. Sharon Milgram, Director, NIH Office of Intramural Training and Education (OITE), National Institutes of Health (NIH), Bethesda, Maryland, USA.

Question 1. would you mind telling us about your background?

I have a PhD in Cellular and Developmental Biology, and worked as a research scientist at the University of North Carolina Chapel Hill, first as a postdoctoral fellow and then as faculty for many years. In 2007, I came to NIH to work as a director of the Office of Intramural Training and Education. The office is a trans-NIH resource for career and professional development of intramural NIH trainees. I also moved my research group at NIH's Heart, Lung and Blood Institute. In my career I have probably mentored around 100 undergraduates, and probably 15 graduate students and postdoctoral fellows. I have mentored many more individuals informally.

Question 2. Do you mind elaborating on what you mean by "informally"?

Informally, students have asked me to be on their thesis committee, and in the department I interacted with a variety of students, in many different disciplines. Now, here at NIH my primary responsibility is talking to fellows to guide them in finding their careers, although this is not the typical kind of mentoring in a research environment.

Question 3. In order to transition at UNC from a research career to this mentoring activity, have you taken courses on education?

No, I do not have any formal training in education, career counseling or career development. However, I have many years of experience in directing programs on those topics and helping individuals to advance their careers by helping them find jobs in different sectors.

Question 4. What type of work do you do, and for how long have you being doing it?

I have directed OITE from 2007, and I oversee training programs, admission recruiting. We establish guidelines for programs and evaluation. We run full sets of courses on career development, and I teach some of them myself. We travel and provide career development for other campuses outside NIH.

Question 5. How many people work in OITE?

OITE has around 24 members and we have some contractors as well. It is a trans-NIH effort.

Question 6. You have been chosen to respond to questions related to the definition of mentoring indicating what mentoring is not. Is that a topic you feel confident about covering?

Yes.

Question 7. Do you think there are specific challenges in the topic of mentoring that need to be addressed?

I do. I think that often in the research environment the words supervisor and mentor are used interchangeably and they should not be. In the research environment there is an inherent tension between both roles. The supervisor is the one who has to make sure that the work gets done properly. The mentor, on the other hand, provides guidance, develops opportunities and guides fellows and students who are in training. It is a topic that is not discussed enough in the research environment. Very often that existing tension is ignored, and more should be done in order to learn how to navigate those tensions. People do not realize how difficult it is to fulfill both roles.

Question 8. Are there any other challenges, particularly in scientific mentoring?

One challenge comes from data showing that many of our trainees will not go on to have independent careers, either by choice or because of the lack of opportunities. Although all of those careers are valuable, they are not appreciated enough by traditionally oriented environments. Having experts in other research environments is a reality, including science communicators, technology experts and educators. Many supervisors in a research environment have narrow views regarding career paths. A major role of mentoring should be to provide direction and guidance through these many possibilities. If someone is interested in industry, we need to provide guidance on how to shape their career to be successful in that field later on. If someone is interested in science policy, that is more distant than a classic scientific research career. The trainee should understand from the start what type of mentoring they should expect and receive, as career mentorship is very important. Mentees should be encouraged to have career mentors. If the supervisor does not have that knowledge, the trainee should look for a career mentor that can guide them.

Another challenge is that perhaps many people do not go into science to develop the next generation of scientists. They want to produce cutting edge science and they focus all their energy, time and creativity towards that goal. Mentoring is thus not a priority. They do not care about developing or acquiring mentoring skills. Since many of our trainees do not follow traditional pathways (or what have been regarded as traditional pathways until now), the best scientists, the brilliant ones, have not received appropriate training as career mentors and lack the skills needed to provide the right kind of mentoring that the new generations need. Therefore, outstanding scientists are not the best of mentors.

Question 9. You may choose not to answer this question, but do you think that mentoring the mentors is needed in those organizations?

You can't make somebody into a good mentor. If it is not on their priority list, if they are involved in many other competing areas, it is irrelevant to require the training. Under those circumstances, there is no point in training mentors. Remember that not everybody goes into science with the desire to manage, mentor and teach. They may prefer to focus in doing outstanding science. This generates a conflict in the institution between the ability of the individual to attract funding and produce good science, and their poor mentoring skills. They generate the science that we all know is important and needs to be produced, but meanwhile young scientists go into the laboratory environment and are not always mentored appropriately.

Question 10. Do you have any strategy for effective monitoring?

These are my strategies in the research environment:

1. First, by being open and transparent regarding grants and funding, and have a clear understanding of needs and priorities. This involves determining the requirements of the mentee, and looking for opportunities to fulfill them. Transparency on the part of the mentor encourages openness in the mentee.

2. My second strategy is to dissociate data analysis and professional assignments, because they are very different areas. Data should go with data, experimental design with experimental design and mentoring conversations with mentoring conversations. One conversation could be about experimental planning. What are you getting from this environment and what aren't you getting from this environment, and how can I help you to achieve your goals? This might involve attending specific courses, or traveling to a scientific meeting. They are different things and should remain separate. A different conversation might be about the future, the best ways their training could help them with their needs for the next step. That can only be achieved by having those conversations. Communicating needs input from both parties.

Question 11. Do you think that there may be reluctance on the part of mentees to disclose to their academic mentors that they are inclined to follow career paths that are not necessarily the traditional ones?

I do not think that is just an issue in more academically oriented institutions. I think it is a problem in any arena. Some people may choose not to talk to their supervisor about their choice of a career. Often, that is more related to the mentee's lack of confidence. That is a mistake, because I think that if you believe in something you should be able to articulate it in a positive way. I think one way to avoid that issue is to urge postdocs to choose carefully the laboratories they are going to work in. Many choose their places based on the science and not on the type of mentoring or the environment they will find there. They should spend some time exploring laboratory dynamics and evaluating what to expect once they move there. They should start by finding a positive environment and then looking at the science.

Question 12. Clearly the track that is most commonly followed at NIH is the classical one. That is a reality of this organization.

I would not agree with that. I think our trainees are informed about and offered a variety of other careers, for example industry, science policy, and education. The culture is not only focused on academic careers. The culture in the laboratory may be only research oriented, but at our office, we provide a wide array of possibilities and knowledge for trainees to examine and consider.

Question 13. Are you aware of the change that your office has brought to this organization on that regard?

Well I was not here before I arrived here! It is hard for me to compare. But I do think having a central office that is very proactive and assertive in providing support for all career paths is a benefit for the intramural program. As I travel and meet people from universities at many national meetings, I receive positive feedback about our courses, videos or programs on the web. Many have mentioned the importance of these resources in the selection of their careers, and it is based on that feedback that I think the impact of this office benefits institutions outside NIH as well. As an example, six people came to me yesterday after a lecture I gave on a different campus, and mentioned that they had watched our videos. They stated that my career symposium had helped them. NIH has a responsibility to be more accessible. I understand that with tight budgets, we need to concentrate on the intramural environment first. The fact that we can produce videos and attend national meetings allows us to reach to the outside world, and I appreciate that part of my job a lot.

Question 14. Is there any change in the traditional practice of mentoring that you would envision to improve the practice in the setting of modern mentoring?
Mentoring committees perhaps will be instrumental on that regard, but I do not have much to say about that.

Question 15. Could you give some specific advice for mentors?
We focus exclusively on science and we try to talk about personal styles or ways to communicate or other topics that are more personal, and it does not necessarily resonate with us in a positive way. Probably that is because we are scientists. It is very good advice to take a deep breath and have an appreciation of who we are and how different we are from each other and learn how to interact better. Feeling more comfortable in spending

time talking about solving conflict, using role play to understand situations, or learning about the different communication styles, will help us to be better mentors, in addition to the personal empowerment. Being relaxed about it and embracing emotional intelligence will help us in understanding ourselves and solving conflict.

Question 16. Where do you think that resistance comes from?

It is particularly prevalent with scientists, because in the past they received inappropriate training or a different type of mentoring. However, many times I have attended bad seminars or workshops, and have still been able to get something out of it. Understanding how different we are from each other and from our trainees is critical.

It is hard for people raised in an upper middle class environment, as many scientists are, to understand or appreciate how much we are asking of the young scientist to develop and grow. Students from disadvantaged backgrounds may already be subject to a lot of pressures, without adding more. We should be aware of this, and more open to learning about these students' lives. Mentors come from well-off communities, and it is hard for them to understand the impact of education and upbringing on young scientists.

Question 17. Do you think there is hope that in the future, we may have a wider demographic of scientists, from all backgrounds?

Only if we continue to train the fellows to develop interpersonal skills and awareness of differences and training on how to be an effective mentor. Without training, people come to an environment and the environment molds them, and what we really want is that the individual molds their environment to suit their needs. Mentoring should be a high priority.

Question 18. Would you provide some words of wisdom for the mentees?

No-one is perfect. Do not put so much emphasis on making your mentor happy every day.

Question 19. Would you say something about the "needy" mentees who come from an environment of pampering?

Needy mentees ... I actually do not think that is a mentoring issue. I think that it is a maturation issue.

Question 20. Would you like to elaborate on the difference between mentoring and supervision?

Supervisors tell people what work to do. They are more concerned on getting the work done than the career development of the individual. Mentors put a lot of energy into developing the individual and that sometimes means the work gets done more slowly.

I also like to draw a distinction between mentoring and friendship. Some students think that mentoring is a very personal relationship, and to some degree it is. However, it is a personal relationship in the professional arena; it is not affection. Some things should be discussed outside the work environment and should be dealt with separately from the mentoring aspects. That said, there is no fine line between what is personal and what is professional. It is important for both to understand that the relationship does not necessarily need to end up in friendship. It might, but this will be a much later development.

Question 21. What is the best way to approach a situation in which you are assigned a supervisor and it is assumed that they will be your mentor?

I think there is a chance of eliminating the tension by having multiple mentors. For graduate students in particular, having a thesis committee early in the game will help provide things that the primary mentor is not supplying, and will also help in "checks and balances." At the level of the postdoctoral fellow, it is a little bit more difficult, because there are no longer the checks and balances of the committee. We (OITE) feel comfortable providing career advice, but not quite so comfortable in providing any type of scientific advice. Working in a very collaborative environment could provide the postdoc with another avenue where more than one person may guide them. In a broader research group, with genuine engagement in a larger collaboration, there is a higher probability of establishing a good mentor—mentee relationship.

Question 22. Moving from the traditional individual focused science to the team science approach represents a gain, correct?

Exactly. That is correct.

Question 23. The pressures on supervisors, mentors and professors increase in times of tight budgets. We are operating in a constrained mode now. In times of scarcity like the present one, the future of the trainees does not look good. Do you have any advice or words of wisdom for them?

We have been in difficult times before. The job market for emerging scientists is changing, I am positive that with the appropriate training, and education about opportunities, and mentorship that provides support, the trainees will find their niches. Prioritizing and compromising will allow us to keep doing great science. Being proactive is the key. Compromise, prioritize, be proactive, and find the right environment.

Question 24. Do you want to add anything else?

Yes, since this book is going to reach other communities outside NIH, I would like to recommend others to read the OITE web page, the career blog, and take advantage of the resources that NIH has to offer (https://www.training.nih.gov).

CHAPTER NOTES AND OBSERVATIONS

In this section, you are welcome to write your notes. You could use the following system, provided that you have some time to dedicate to it.

First, just write, do not worry about processing. Just write the first thing that comes to your mind. Use this space to do it. Extend the writing as much as you want or simply write one sentence, or even perhaps just one word. We will call that section *Brainstorming*.

In the second section, you are invited to reflect. The section will be your space to elaborate more about your brainstorming to organize the thoughts and make sense of them. That second section will be called *Reflection*. Although you can work on that section immediately after you have finished your brainstorming, it is advisable to come back to it later, the next day or even a week or two after the brainstorming took place. Unlike the first section, this second one will call for a more organized style of writing, where the brainstorming ideas crystallize to form concepts that you own, that you generated from yourself. Note that those concepts could align with the reading, or differ from it. It does not matter. Those are the concepts you generated through your own elaboration.

Finally, you can summarize, perhaps with the help of bullet points or short sentences, the most outstanding ideas or concepts from the topic. That section, typically shorter than the former ones will be named *Conclusion*.

I invite you to start with this chapter.

Brainstorming

Reflection

Conclusion

_____

_____

_____

_____

_____

_____

_____

CHAPTER 3

Mentoring Outreach—The Multiplicative Effect

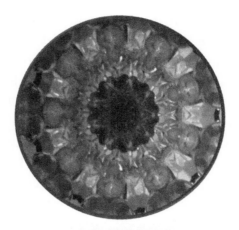

The mentoring relationship produces mutual satisfaction. When mentoring has been successful both parties feel comfortable and experience gratitude. Experiencing gratitude often leads mentees to increase their needs to transfer their experience to others, generating a chain effect that results in a multiplicative effect. The best mentors are those who have received successful mentoring.

THE POWER OF GRATITUDE—EXERCISE

The need to transfer gratitude once it has been received is immediate, almost instinctive. In many of my workshops I ask the attendees

Interdisciplinary Mentoring in Science
DOI: http://dx.doi.org/10.1016/B978-0-12-415962-4.00003-5
© 2014 Elsevier Inc.
All rights reserved.

to take a couple of minutes to think about an event in which somebody has been kind to them and has provided something that awoken a feeling of gratitude on them. It is very interesting to observe the audience at that moment, and to detect a big smile on almost every face. I elaborate more on that, stating that the event does not need to be in a scientific setting, it could have been when they were young or even that morning, when they entered the building and someone held the door or smiled to them. Once they are content with their memories I asked them to center and try to experience in their bodies the feeling of gratitude, to recreate at that precise instant the deep satisfaction they went through then. The energy of the room is building at this time and I move forward with the exercise, requesting them to pair and share their experiences with each other while trying to keep the feeling alive. Invariably, I have to make an effort to stop them 5 or 10 minutes later, because everybody wants to continue talking. This is a very energizing and powerful exercise; I recommend that you try it, and advice others to do it. I also recommend it for those situations in which one feels frustrated or particularly down, because re-experiencing a feeling of that nature is very healing and nurturing. Try it.

Once the exercise is over, everybody is engaged and ready to receive more information, their minds opened and their attention full; in addition, everyone is smiling and looks wonderful.

In any example you find, either yours or from others, there is a common pattern; the need to reciprocate. This is a need that mobilizes us to give back to the individual who originally offered the kindness or to anybody else who crosses our path when we are in the giving-back mode. There is then a complex web of individuals who are interconnected by acts of kindness and gratitude that in turn will result in new acts of kindness and generate new expressions of gratitude—you get the picture.

Mentoring is a relationship largely based on the power of gratitude. Starting with the concept that mentors give without expecting anything in return, just the satisfaction of seeing a mentee grow and develop as an integral person is enough. The generosity of mentors is probably what develops a sense of gratitude in their mentees. That is why when those mentees become mentors in turn, they are ready to give back. I contend that the best mentors are those who received good mentoring. I do not know if the opposite is true, though.

It is easy to imagine a world in which the transfer of gratitude in the way of mentoring starts spreading into different niches, offering opportunities to transform relationships, organizations, the whole scientific community, perhaps. That was the hope behind the efforts of some of my colleagues in Latin America, when we decided to engage scientists in a new form of mentoring that would translate into much more effective collaborations and training.

A community that engages in good mentoring is a community that:

- has positive values
- exercises good ethical practices
- grows in collegiality
- collaborates freely
- makes competition a positive value and not a negative one
- supports each other
- generates flexible minds, and much more.

If members of those communities initiate their own practices of mentoring, their new territories will be fertile soil in which those principles will be sown, and new mentalities and forms of collaboration will be born. Then it is not impossible to imagine that a new community of positive thinkers could be built, based on the principles of good mentoring practices.

That is the power of the multiplicative effect of gratitude. To illustrate this phenomenon and to dissipate the doubts from the incredulous minds of the scientists who may attend my workshops, I tell them a story. I bring to my talks a children's book called *A Grain of Rice*. It is a book often categorized as a "mathematical tale." The version I take with me has beautiful illustrations and it is very engaging. If you want to be surprised by the tale, and read it yourself from the book, do not read the next paragraph; if you are curious about it, here it is.

The story takes place in a faraway town in India, where a powerful king was very selfish and only cared about himself. He made the people collect rice and he stored the grains for himself in case it became scarce.

One year later, the rice crop failed and he was the only one who had something to eat. Elephants were passing by with many bags containing rice on the roads to the king's palace, and the poor people had to look at them while starving.

One girl, called Rani, noticed that one of the bags being transported was leaking and immediately went to collect the rice that was falling on the ground. A guard saw her and accused her of stealing from the king. Rani, a very sharp girl, fearing for her life said she was collecting the rice to return it to the king. The guard believed her and took her in front of the king so she could tell him her story. The king, pleasantly surprised, thanked her and also offered her the possibility to ask for a wish that he said he would grant.

Rani did not hesitate, and said: "Well, dear king, I would like one grain of rice today, tomorrow I would like two, double that the next day, and so on for 30 days. The king was not sure that it was a good choice to grant that wish but agreed to grant it if that was what she wanted. It did not take long for the king to start having second thoughts about his concession, since every day the number of bags of rice started to increase rapidly, with double the next day and double the day after that. If you think, you can get the picture; imagine the people looking at the book, and seeing pages folded on their own that have to be opened up to observe the many camels carrying bags of rice! In case anyone is still skeptical after this demonstration of geometrical progression, I show them the calculations posted at the end of the book in a matrix starting at 1 and ending in number 536,870,912; at the end of 30 days, the total amount of rice reaches a value of 1,073,741,823, more than a billion grains of rice!

That is why the effort of best mentoring practice may start in any place, at any moment, but the principles will disseminate with time and more and more people will be part of a web of mentoring.

I invite you to be part of the multiplicative effect, today. Involve as many as you can and be sure the power of gratitude is propagated.

OUTREACH

As mentioned before, outreach in mentoring is immeasurable. The effect of good mentoring will translate into good mentoring to others, and so on. This is the case with many mentors who cannot imagine that their actions today may impact indirectly on many others. It is one of those effects that can be predicted or imagined, but probably never confirmed. The mentor transcends. Their words of wisdom, advice, encouragement, and support, although intended to help one individual's development, reach many more people via the multiplicative effect. It is for that reason that the role of the mentor deserves extra attention. The mentor is the role model of many, not only the mentee. People are watching, observing, paying close attention; moreover, mentors are constantly setting examples. Once the mentor becomes a role model, those elements that are appreciated by others are adopted by the observers, who will, in turn, transfer them to a new generation of mentees or observers.

Mentoring Outreach in the Interdisciplinary Setting

(Since the concept of I-Mentoring will be developed in full in Chapter 5, the reader will be presented here with a brief mention of outreach, to be re-visited again in that chapter.)

The outreach of classical mentoring practice was described above. It is tempting to translate the effect of good mentoring from the classical to the interdisciplinary setting. In such situations, one mentor is exposed to many mentees and will impact many individuals simultaneously. Hence, the multiplication of good mentoring practice will be much more prolific and the outreach immense. The I-Mentor (Interdisciplinary-Mentor), although mentoring a group rather than specific individuals, will be a role model for many. They become the role model, the individual who possesses many of the qualities summarized in Chapter 5. Even when the I-Mentor focus should be the group, the group will be focusing on the mentor at times when needs arise that can be attended only by them.

Outreach in the interdisciplinary setting cannot be measured; mentoring practices transcend the group and impact many others, beyond the original setting. The I-Mentor is the multiplier.

A WORD OF CAUTION

Because we are all working on the topic of mentoring, we are connected by positive thoughts and assume that we are discussing good mentoring. However, we all know that mentoring can be bad or non-existent. Both instances can drive mentees to frustration, deception, anger, and negativity. Since people with such characteristics are also observed and taken as examples by others, a word of caution is necessary. Individuals who have not received mentoring are typically non-believers. These may include teachers, professors, CEOs, chiefs, and directors. Such individuals are going to be hard to convince regarding the need of mentoring, and the importance of mentoring programs. They may even say: "I did not receive any mentoring and I am CEO of such and such prestigious company or institution." That phrase is analogous to the smoker who argues that his uncle smoked all his life and never had lung cancer!

It is hard to deal with such individuals. However, confronting them or fighting their positions will not be beneficial. Instead, people need to be told that times are different, that new generations need to be approached with other elements in hand, and that the science itself is different and needs to be approached in a way that aligns with modern times.

Since in the interdisciplinary setting everyone is a player and has to be invited to the table, it is critical for the interaction and articulation of the group to consider all positions and points of view.

> *People who have not received mentoring or have received poor mentoring may appear skeptical, but they should participate, observe, and perhaps learn about the practices described in this book and many others, and they may even eventually adopt them.*

OBSTACLES

Reality knocks at the door and all the good intentions become just that—intentions. Recognizing that there are obstacles to applying the concepts described above is a responsible thing to do. Some obstacles will be discussed here, and potential solutions or approaches to those hurdles will be offered.

Lack of Support from the Mainstream

The practice of mentoring is an old art, it dates from Ancient Greece, and it has been an essential tool of artists, professionals, thinkers, masters, and almost everyone else. That is not under discussion; what we are focusing on here, and what could be questioned by some, is the new form of mentoring. The new mentoring involves an approach that is less vertical, and generates relationships that are permanent and defined on the bases of communication and trust rather than hierarchies and imposition. Many will agree with that, some will disagree. Most of the resistance will came from fear. People resist new things almost as a reflex. They will go on to state that: "things have been done like this (referring about the traditional path) for more than 20 years, we are not going to change now." Fear of the new approach is the truth. People feel comfortable with "A" because they know "A." Why are they going to change to "B" now? They need to learn together with others and be willing to abandon their comfort zone, where they have reigned as leaders for many years and have been regarded as authorities in their field.

One option for dealing with this is to be persistent. Do not antagonize or treat such people as anachronistic. Be prepared to engage the resistant ones, particularly if they make decisions that will impact the future of a mentoring effort. Often, there is one person who buys into a new idea; partner with that person and then ask them to help you invite others. The resistant individual will be more prone to participate if one of their peers invites them.

Skepticism

Skeptical and cynical comments are going to plague your meetings and discussions. Being prepared to deal with those is paramount. People in general are resistant to believing, and much less embracing, the unknown. You, on the other hand, will already be convinced, and base your beliefs in your own experiences as a mentee and a mentor. However, sometimes being convinced and having the "data" often required by scientists to validate a hypothesis is not enough. Accept comments and put them aside, unless they are questions that require answers. If a negative comment impairs the flow of communication in the meeting you are leading or the activity you are trying to set up, tell the person who brought it up that their idea is also valid and it is a possibility. There are not two opposite schools of thought that contradict each other; everyone can be convivial and harmonize, until people have a chance to understand, embrace, and elaborate concepts. The Arbinger Institute has published a book called *Leadership and Self-Deception* that is especially applicable to situations like the one described above. According to this book, people tend to put themselves inside boxes and they try not to move from them, although they may claim they do. Understanding the proposed concepts in the book will give you tools to handle those who like to stay inside their box. They should be recommended to read it too.

The Challenge of Working with Scientists

Scientists think all the time. They think when they sleep, they think while they shower, they solve their research questions while golfing, swimming, or watching a movie. The brain of a scientist does not rest. Although this is a generalization, most of the time it applies to all scientists around us, including ourselves, as we read this book. We do not realize how technical and data driven we have become, until we are placed in a multidisciplinary setting and share ideas with others who have a different approach to interpreting the truth. Most scientists operate in an intellectual mode. Some of them feel secure in that world, because it is a known area, it is like living in their own house. When invited to take other paths, they are afraid to succumb, to lose their anchors and to become less secure. Even more, when asked to abandon, even for a brief moment, their intellectual self and allow the affective one to emerge, they resist. Most scientists feel debilitated by this. There is a feeling of vulnerability that surfaces along with expressing of emotions, and allowing others to learn about them. Sharing emotions involves an even higher degree of vulnerability that just a select few will be willing to accept. Understanding that *a priori* will help us in conducting activities with scientists. In many cases when I have prepared talks on mentoring directed to biomedical researchers I have had to be very cautious about introducing some concepts, to avoid resistance and rolling eyes. Sensing the audience constantly is one of my ways to address the state of mind of individuals; introducing new concepts slowly is another way to encourage acceptance.

Interestingly, I have been presenting in front of "mixed" audiences, with traditional mentors and young people. It has been very revealing to observe their body language while reacting to some topics, wriggling and restless for some, and nodding their heads for others.

> *Engaging scientists in new concepts of mentoring foreign to their traditional experiences is challenging. If that is done in groups, sense your audience constantly, so as not to lose their attention or annoy them.*

WHAT THE EXPERTS HAVE TO SAY

Interview with Dr. Betty Eidemiller, Education Director at the Society of Toxicology.

Question 1. Would you mind telling us about your background?

I have an undergraduate degree in biology and a PhD in ecology and evolutionary biology, and I taught undergraduate biology for a number of years for small liberal arts colleges and two-year institutions. For the past 17 years, I have been serving on the staff of scientific societies, primarily involved with education programs for K-12 students, undergraduates, graduates, postdocs and strategic programming for the Society of Toxicology.

Question 2. What type of work do you do and for how long have you being doing it?

My answer to Question 1 summarizes what I have been doing.

Question 3. You have been chosen to respond to questions related to mentoring outreach. Is that a topic you feel confident about covering?

Well, not really, but I have been fortunate to be in a situation where there have been multiple opportunities for society members to engage in activities that are very supportive of the personal and professional development of our members and those involved in Society of Toxicology programs.

Question 4. Do you think there are specific challenges in the topic of mentoring outreach that need to be addressed?

I think one of the challenges that everybody faces in this modern age is the time to establish and keep a mentoring relationship. We all have productivity challenges, "do, do, do." Working out what we need to do next is hard. Being deliberate and spending time mentoring others is something that comes naturally for some, but for others it is not like that. The intention has to be there, but also follow-through.

Question 5. Do you think that the contemporary situation of funding and cuts will impose even more restrictions on time for potential mentors?

Yes I do. I would agree with that. Time spent in mentoring relationships might not be considered central to work responsibilities, especially when many professionals are expected to increase productivity with freezing hires or downsizing.

Question 6. Do you have any strategy for obtaining support to mentor minorities effectively?

Commitment has to be there for whoever is sponsoring or supporting the activity that has mentoring as a focus. Commitment should be part of both sides of the equation, ideally with the support of the mentor's employer. The person who takes the responsibility to serve as a mentor needs to be fully committed to find the time to provide mentoring. The mentee needs to engage with the mentor in a way that does not demand too much time and does not result in an imposition. Most people like to share their experiences and insights, so there is benefit to both members of the mentoring pair. But again, finding time and knowing when is the right moment and what is the right approach for people to talk to each other is sometimes difficult and even more so if there are cultural differences. Open and considerate communication is important.

Question 7. Is there any change in the traditional practice of mentoring that you envision will improve practice in the setting of mentoring underprivileged trainees?

Fortunately, people are much more aware of the mechanisms that improve outcomes in mentoring relationships and are really benefiting from learning and using effective strategies. Informed mentors and mentees can enrich their interactions by recognizing differences in backgrounds, gender, etc., building from there and polishing skills useful in the multicultural work place. In addition, no-one is going to move along a career track that is linear. That is the modern professional world, and so people need to look for mentoring in different places to support different areas of professional growth. In an interdisciplinary world, it is crucial to have a variety of skills and be able to participate effectively in many different situations. The traditional academic is no longer the mainstream; people today need to understand how to train students in careers different from their own.

Question 8. Many need to understand that now a lot of graduates will move in what has been termed "alternative careers," a very unfortunate term to define non-traditional or non-bench careers. What would you say about that?

I think NIH was very clear about that in the recent Biomedical Workforce report, where they cited data that the majority of PhD graduates are not going to embark on a traditional academic research career. Therefore, the mentor needs to help trainees discover alternatives that fit the interests and skills of the particular individual and are promising career directions; the mentor and the mentee may not be aware of these options without some exploration.

Question 9. Since you are the founder of the undergraduate program of the Committee on Diversity Initiatives (CDI) of the Society of Toxicology, would you mind explaining how the program operates?

First of all let me clarify that Marion Ehrich is the founder of the SOT undergraduate program. My staff role began later after the program was well-established, and it has been an extreme privilege to help structure that program along the way. The program has the objective of supporting students coming from a variety of backgrounds, where opportunities are not abundant and exposure to research is not very common. The background of many minority students is such that they are only aware of traditional careers such as being a lawyer or a medical doctor. Therefore, during the annual meeting of the Society of Toxicology the undergraduate students, typically with backgrounds in biology, are arranged in small groups, constituted by four students, graduate student peer mentors, faculty advisors, and toxicologist host mentors who have meals together and share multiple activities organized in the course of three days. The sessions include a formal introduction to toxicology through lectures, attendance at poster sessions, interactions with poster presenters, and also speaking with graduate students about attending graduate school, and interacting with program directors, who can assist with what is needed to produce a successful graduate school application. Promotion of awareness of internships, key activities that promote people into careers in biomedical research, is also included in the program. Mentors follow up after the program with members in their groups. The students who are most proactive in keeping up a relationship with their mentors derive the most benefit from the program. They obtain advice on how to get internships, select the best fit for graduate school, and other possibilities for their careers. These students have been effectively utilizing the resources presented to them. Following up on the relationships they have established during the meeting has been proven to be extremely beneficial for them.

Question 10. Would you say that this has been a successful program, even without the metrics in front of you?

We do. It is difficult to accumulate a large number of program participants who ultimately obtain a PhD in biomedical sciences, especially when the baseline number of minority students entering biomedical graduate school is unfortunately so small. However, the Society of Toxicology boasts a number of active members from groups under-represented in the sciences who first encountered the discipline during this undergraduate program. In addition, we have increased awareness of a very important science and we have highlighted opportunities that students may have not considered previously. Sometimes students circle back in their careers and reassess and rethink at a later time. Another important successful aspect is the mentoring that is taking place among members of the committee, organizers of the program, graduate student peer mentors, and academic program directors, who work together every year. A valuable cross-fertilization goes on in the program itself.

Question 11. Can you give some specific advice for mentors?

I think that having energetic, inspirational leaders is very important. Having good role models is essential for each of us. It is especially important for minority students to have the opportunity to interact with someone successful in the career path who may be like them. Being a role model is rewarding. Beyond what can be done individually, being part of a program that is intentional and well thought out, with a dedicated team using proven techniques, generating deliberate actions to support people, that is going to have an impact. Understand that even if the mentee does not follow the pathway that the mentor might advocate, there is still potential for personal growth and satisfaction for both.

Question 12. You mean it is important when the effort comes from the heart, right? When there is a genuine desire to move forward the career of others, correct?

That is very well put, "when it comes from the heart." Then a mentor will be inspirational.

Question 13. Can you provide some words of wisdom for mentees?

Mentees need to be courageous and talk to their mentors, not just wait. The mentee needs to be considerate with the mentor, but also be bold and use the communication channels that are open to them.

Question 14. Culturally, in Hispanic communities, for instance, that is something we need to work on. We are typically shy. What would you say?

I think you are right in that the cultural aspects have an impact on communication, and more so if the two don't share the same culture. Having direct conversations about the most effective ways to communicate will work in favor of the relationship. The mentor needs to understand there might be reluctance to "impose" and find ways to draw out the mentee, and the mentee will need to practice being more forward.

Question 15. Anything else you would like to add?

You have great questions. I am very happy to have contributed to this work which will help foster good mentoring relationships.

CHAPTER NOTES AND OBSERVATIONS

In this section, you are welcome to write your notes. You could use the following system, provided that you have some time to dedicate to it.

First, just write, do not worry about processing. Just write the first thing that comes to your mind. Use this space to do it. Extend the writing as much as you want or simply write one sentence, or even perhaps just one word. We will call that section *Brainstorming*.

In the second section, you are invited to reflect. The section will be your space to elaborate more about your brainstorming to organize the thoughts and make sense of them. That second section will be called *Reflection*. Although you can work on that section immediately after you have finished your brainstorming, it is advisable to come back to it later, the next day or even a week or two after the brainstorming took place. Unlike the first section, this second one will call for a more organized style of writing, where the brainstorming ideas crystallize to form concepts that you own, that you generated from yourself. Note that those concepts could align with the reading, or differ from it. It does not matter. Those are the concepts you generated through your own elaboration.

Finally, you can summarize, perhaps with the help of bullet points or short sentences, the most outstanding ideas or concepts from the topic. That section, typically shorter than the former ones will be named *Conclusion*.

I invite you to start with this chapter.

Brainstorming

_____

_____

_____

_____

_____

_____

_____

Reflection

_____

_____

_____

_____

_____

_____

_____

Conclusion

_____

CHAPTER 4

Mentoring Minorities and Women

In an interdisciplinary research community, diversity is one parameter to be aware of. Not only international collaborations involve foreign nationals. Currently, the scientific landscape of a modern laboratory comprises multiple ethnicities, languages, cultures and religions. It is of great value for teams to be able to count on diverse opinions and approaches to solve scientific enigmas.

Mentoring minorities is a task that requires extra skills: flexibility, openness, learning, sympathizing, and respect.

WHY DIVERSITY?

Perhaps it would be advisable to agree on a definition of diversity, or at least the concept of diversity that will be used in

Interdisciplinary Mentoring in Science
DOI: http://dx.doi.org/10.1016/B978-0-12-415962-4.00004-7

© 2014 Elsevier Inc.
All rights reserved. 63

this book. Since the term could be interpreted from many different perspectives, I shall attempt to introduce one interpretation.

Often a diverse environment is understood as the one that posses "acceptance" of individuals of different background, e.g. race, ethnicity, gender, sexual orientation, socio-economic status, age, physical abilities, religious beliefs, and political beliefs. There is a difference between mere tolerance, and acceptance and embracing. In many cases companies, academic units, or other organizations include some degree of diversity in their workforces because they have to, and not necessarily because they either accept it, or much less embrace it.

As the reader realizes, there is a large discrepancy in the outcome for organizations that embrace diversity and consider that a critical asset in their development, and those that do it because it is imposed or it has to be done.

Analysis of those situations will follow.

EXAMPLE OF IMPOSED DIVERSITY IN THE WORKFORCE

As with any imposed situation, this is not a good thing. Supervisors who are forced to select their employees based on criteria they do not believe in are usually unhappy and not completely satisfied with the situation. In this case, the entire environment will be unwelcoming to the unfortunate person who has been selected to work there. The outcome is obvious; the person will not feel welcomed, and will fail and leave. The results will be defined as "not a good match," and the organization will search for another unfortunate candidate, to justify their compliance with imposed regulations. Leaders who act on these principles are not successful in generating an environment of cooperation, and will usually fail at running an organization that matures and grows.

Another example is that of institutions or organizations that comply with rules that are not written down, but which they have been advised to follow. Those organizations, as the individuals defined above, will also fail because they do not understand the value of diversity, and how they will improve their development as institutions and their magnitude and outreach by embracing diversity in their workforce.

The dynamic of real acceptance (as opposed to mere tolerance) is dramatically different than the situations described. Embracing implies a real involvement in the incorporation of individuals with different backgrounds. Although not an easy experience, interacting and working as a close group with individuals who are diverse requires a change in attitude and flexibility of mind from everybody.

In future chapters, the concept of interactions in an interdisciplinary setting will be discussed and the reader will find some parallelisms between acceptance of diversity and the creation and sustainability of interdisciplinary groups.

CULTURAL MIX

It is a common misconception to believe that when we talk about cultural mix, we are referring to mixtures that involve different languages or costumes. It is believed that acceptance implies eating and appreciating foreign food! However, it is relatively rare to understand that "codes" embedded in different cultures could interfere with personal interactions. Because codes are non-written rules, and because clues are not always perceived by those who are not familiar with a specific culture, considerable thought should be dedicated to the topic. Individuals who are truly interested in embracing diversity will need to work in an environment where everybody feels able to express their thoughts without judgment. Cultural clichés have to be accepted from everybody as normal and not as far from the norm. Exercising respect and trust for instance, will produce a much more relaxed environment. This process takes time, but the outcome is a very rewarding one.

Communication in the Cultural Mix

Consider communication as one of the most important elements in a group. What is communication for a modern occidental society, or corporations based on occidental models of organization? Basically, it is a system by which individuals impart opinions to each other, either verbal or written. In some instances that mechanism is used to articulate solutions to challenges presented by the everyday running of business. However, cultural difference plays a critical role in the concept of communication, as it is understood by occidental organizations. In some cultures, communicating a different point of view to a superior is an almost impossible task. For others, being direct to superiors is a very common way of communication. The middle ground will be comfortable only for those who are used to making their messages polite. A system needs to be in place to understand these differences, and to help those who are afraid to communicate, as well as to "polish" the contributions of those who are rather too direct in their speech. Understanding each other in a diverse community takes one important factor: interest. If all members are interested in communicating, then the messages will be heard and understood. Members should understand that body language may be read and processed, ignored, or over-interpreted. It is not infrequent to be part of a group in which some members do not establish eye contact, and body language for those members will be non-existent. In contrast, those individuals who are not familiar with the language of the team will be more prone to base their understanding on body language than the spoken word.

LEADERSHIP AND EMBRACING OF DIVERSITY

The role of the leader in this process is critical, and should be an example to be followed by others. As in many aspects of the optimization of the groups or organizations, the leader should be a role model. If the leader embraces diversity and excels in interacting with others, then interactions among members of the group will be easier. The process of appreciation of new ideas divergent from the classical ones requires a considerable maturity and self-esteem. It is in the best interest of leaders, and the organizations they lead, to accept these qualities and adopt them for discussion and potential incorporation. Accepting ideas that move us from our comfort zone requires resolution and results in a big move towards creativity.

GENDER

It should not come as a surprise that in some cultures, men and women are not treated equally. That situation will have implications in communication among members of any organization that is inclusive and accepts diversity. Being a male coming from a male-dominated society can put individuals in awkward situations when speaking to women. If women coming from those societies are put in positions of leadership or need to communicate with men at lower levels of the organization, the opposite will occur. Gender bias is still a challenge in many organizations, although not a topic for discussion in this book. However, given the importance of trust and respect in the setting of interdisciplinary research groups and the relevance of mentoring in those settings, a dedicated section to the mentoring of women is included.

MENTORING WOMEN

The Impostor Syndrome

Crushing self-doubt experienced by almost any successful woman has been defined by Clance and Imes as the "impostor syndrome" or "impostor phenomenon." Although not exclusive to women, the syndrome is more prevalent in women. It has been described in depth by Valerie Young as based on self-questioning, doubts about abilities and a deep feeling of incompetence. The impostor syndrome probably arises from old misconceptions and continuous remarks about women's place in society, and the role of women as mothers and housewives *versus* career-oriented individuals. Even the most successful women fear sometimes that they will be "discovered," and that they have reached their positions or won awards or recognition by consistently fooling people as to their abilities. These thoughts induce deep anxiety and uneasiness that is translated into suboptimal performance, and also sometimes physical symptoms. Mentoring women, then, implies an extra step of communication and advice on how to replace concerns by facts. A good approach to working with women suffering from the impostor syndrome is to ask them to find a quiet place at night, before going to sleep, when all the thoughts of the day come together, and start a list called "list AB," for abilities. On that list, they need to compile all the abilities they have, even if minimal (or considered minimal by their standards).

I once had a conversation with a female co-worker in which I suggested that she compile such a list. Among the examples of items I asked her to include was her extremely good spoken English. It never occurred to her, a woman of Asian descent, that speaking good English would be a plus. After a short explanation of why that could be a plus for a female Asian scientist who needs to communicate on a regular basis, she acknowledged it and immediately started to feel better about herself. That list is a dynamic document that can grow every day. Once the person feels that the list is sufficiently long, a second list should be initiated, named "list AC" for accomplishments. This list is perhaps harder for women to generate. Women are much more reluctant to accept that they have accomplished something. They are reluctant to even recognize events as accomplishments. That is why *resumés* or *curriculum vitae* have to be constantly "revisited" by others, to help women highlight their real strengths. Once both lists are written, the women will feel much better about themselves, and they will gain a feeling of entitlement. Sometimes generation of the lists needs some help or coaching from others. Women joining an interdisciplinary setting need to understand and cope with the impostor syndrome. Their role as members of a team will require consistent interaction and empowerment to be able to handle collaborations. It is therefore essential that women are coached to produce a favorable outcome before they become part of a team.

Self-Esteem

A related event to the impostor syndrome is the low self-esteem which is experienced by many women. Based on cultural beliefs and background, women often feel unable to accept challenges and are slow to take risks. In a society where guilt is associated with success, envy is often part of the equation. Hence, women will be singled out if they are successful by pointing out to them how many hours they spend away from the home. Often this accusation comes from individuals (men and women) who were not courageous enough themselves to take risks, and who chose to remain protected under the umbrella of familiar obligations. Even those women with high self-esteem will be hesitant and doubtful of themselves if presented with criticism about their decision to work instead of raising children. The input of a coach or a mature colleague will be helpful in giving some clarity and providing advice to help reinforce decisions.

Self-esteem is usually harmed by inner thoughts, although often external comments may also awake doubts and questioning.

It is extremely important that women enter the interdisciplinary world after having had some prior coaching or mentoring experience that has provided elements to deal with this issue. In the collaborative setting, it is not uncommon to find scientists who consider their disciplines more relevant or critical to the development of the common project. On many occasions, male colleagues from the "hard" sciences will consider other scientific disciplines minor or secondary, and will be able to convey this message with very subtle comments and attitudes. Women will be perceptive and sensitive to these, and their self-esteem will be fractured; just as fractures produced by earthquakes, they will progress and spread in multiple branches. The outcome will not be a happy one.

Competition and Misconceptions

Women usually have to work more than men to "prove themselves." In general, women need to spend more hours just to be as visible as men are in front of their supervisors. It is not uncommon to find that it is expected that women stay home if a child is ill, or take days off if a family member needs help, and that absences are more frequent for mothers to attend school functions or parent–teacher conferences. Such assumptions generate a "guilt" feeling that provokes extra anxiety each time the phone rings and there is a call from house or school. Men know that, and they also assume that their visibility is more pre-eminent. If a position is offered, they may feel that they are much more deserving because they are more reliable. After all, they can work long hours and play golf with their bosses!

This burden, added to the inconsistency in salaries between genders, drives women to a state of semi-insanity, with persistent negative messages gravitating around them. Even so, performance is never affected and women keep producing and delivering according to the high standards they impose on themselves. Today, more women are embarking on scientific careers, and reports and statistics reflect that. However, the field is still dominated by men. It is not uncommon to see the faces of elderly men in suits representing the executive boards of many scientific societies. Those figures are still the ones who are regarded as leaders in the field, and the most accepted characters in our contemporary scientific community. The process of blending other talented individuals into the mix is taking longer than expected. Nobody wants to let go of power, and women have fewer advocates. Not only that, women must be very strong to survive and be treated as equals on executive boards or committees composed of men. That is why it is so important to pave the way for women, by interacting with them frequently and empowering them, showing them their abilities and skills beyond the "nibble effect" generated by others (Kaleel Jamison has written on this topic in *The Nibble Theory and the Kernel of Power: A Book About Leadership, Self-Empowerment, and Personal Growth*).

Mentoring women is a topic that has been developed extensively for the business environment, but not so much for the scientific setting. One of the most comprehensive books I encountered on the topic has been written by Emily Wadsworth, in her book *Giving Much, Gaining More*. In that work, she compiles real stories from women enrolled in the engineering program at Purdue University. The author uses the concept of polarity to describe each story, producing a real impact on the reader and generating natural empathy. Dr. Wadsworth summarizes the experiences of her graduates in 12 polarities that I have decided to list because they are very relevant for the scientific community. She defines them as: welcoming *vs.* excluding; communicating *vs.* bickering; trusting *vs.* doubting; accepting *vs.* rejecting; affirming *vs.* ridiculing; forgiving *vs.* condemning; reframing *vs.* stagnating; letting go *vs.* holding tight; rejoicing *vs.* grieving; balancing *vs.* tilting; focusing *vs.* blurring; and gracing *vs.* alienating.

A Word of Caution

It is not unknown that each time the topic of gender is brought up in front of a diverse audience, reactions are mixed. While half of the audience will nod in agreement with the comments presented regarding inequalities, the other half will be ready to leave the room, looking at their watches and wriggling in their chairs. I do not need to explain what gender is likely to compose each half!

> *In order to generate a comprehensive collaborative community, both men and women need to communicate their fears, their expectations and their goals.*
>
> *It is important for both genders to reach agreement and to coincide in elemental practices to be able to reach consensus and to generate a work environment where talent and creativity flourish and thrive. A good leader and mentor of a group should be exquisitely sensitive to these details, and try to start from scratch from both sides and minimize differences or unbalanced situations that would generate unhappiness.*

MENTORING MINORITIES

This is an extremely complex issue to discuss. However, it would not be fair to our many minority scientists and future scientists to skip it.

During my career as a biomedical researcher, I have focused particularly on minority mentoring. It was not difficult for me to understand and communicate with Hispanics, and it was not hard to understand the fears and caveats of many African—Americans when research was their choice.

As such, I immediately realized that empowering minorities in science was more than a task, it was a moral obligation.

Many minority students and young scientists in general suffer from the impostor syndrome (see above), not only because they do not feel qualified, but also because they feel "they do not belong." Engrained in the minds of many Hispanic students are the common phrases repeated by many regarding the lack of jobs for Americans that are now in hands of Hispanics. Latinos feel they are stealing from their native counterparts their opportunities to work and succeed. It is not uncommon to observe many of the minority students stepping aside when an opportunity is presented to them. It has taken me many hours to convince my mentees to apply for a travel award to attend a conference, or a fellowship offered in a scientific journal. They typically react as if that is not intended to be for them, and they interpret all the opportunities as if they are intended for someone else. It is a task for the future to cultivate a spirit of participation by removing the misconceptions feeding the "stealing syndrome."

In the past, many Hispanics were limited to tasks that were not considered prestigious. That image has been perpetuated in the minds of many and it is a common place to associate Hispanics with laborers or janitors. It will be a stretch for many to imagine a Hispanic judge, a physicist, or a NASA engineer, for instance. The landscape of our universities is very different today. The daughters and sons of the janitors and laborers attended college as the first in their families, two or three generations ago. Our work force has seen graduates from many academic institutions with last names that were not the common ones before. Why, therefore, is the mentality of our society still fixated in the past and the stigmatization still persistent?

Stigmatization

I have seen female Hispanic students mortified by the decisions they have made about pursuing a career in science, not only because of the discrimination they suffer from their teachers and peers, but also from their own family members and communities.

Traditionally, the expectation for a Hispanic woman is to be married and be a stay-home mother. Many family members will exert pressure on women who have chosen different pathways that diverge from the traditional. Hence, Hispanic women receive disapproval from their close relatives, often their own mothers, who had envisioned their daughters following the classical path that they had dreamed of. In addition, they have few role models. They are taking a path that is unfamiliar to many of their close friends, cousins or neighbors, so they live in isolation.

> *Hispanic females need to be reminded constantly that they belong, they can do it, they are talented, they will be able to return to their communities with their degrees, they will help their peers, they will be recognized and not ostracized.*

And what about the men? Although they also receive disapproval for choosing to be apart from their typical role, they seem to be able to move forward more easily than women. Hispanic men are also expected to start a family and provide, not to spend their lives studying or doing experiments in a laboratory or teaching. There is also fear that getting a higher education will distance them from their roots, as if education will generate a sense of superiority that will make them grow apart. The lack of role models is also important in this situation. However, now more and more young Hispanics are attending colleges and there are more role models available for the Hispanic community. The role of counselors at school cannot be understated here. Counselors assume that Hispanics have to attend two-year college education, because it is all they can afford. If it is considered that they do not have parents who understand the system, and have never attended school in this country, the disadvantage is exponential. They have to be offered the same possibilities as the rest of the students, regardless of their last name, or the little square box they checked regarding race. Presenting them with all the options as real possibilities, fear and the stealing syndrome will not be obstacles to progress. Unfortunately, counselors play a critical role and they are not sensitive. It has been seen often how they assume instead of giving chances.

One word of encouragement from a counselor is all a student needs to move forward and be successful.

African—Americans

Similar connotations apply for African—Americans. Similar misconceptions and years of discrimination still fall on their shoulders. Although they do not have the burden of being immigrants and the feeling of stealing from other citizens, they also experience pressure from their family and peers. The students often feel that they have "abandoned" their families because they are growing apart, taking a different path that is not aligned with the classical one. Role models are not abundant, and they feel separated from their friends, relatives, and communities. Discrimination starts at school; even in those environments created to generate a mixed population of students, such as magnet programs, it is not unusual to observe separation and gathering according to race. Teachers also play a critical role. It is common for teachers to pay more attention to, and have higher expectations of, non-minority students, generally Caucasians and Orientals. As such, minority students are rarely pushed to the limit, and teachers are pleased if they achieve less than their counterparts even if that is only a fraction of their potential.

As a consequence, minority students of African descent are typically not pushed to the limit, not asked to perform like their peers to their maximum potential, and are often viewed as outliers by their families and friends if they chose a different path. Success is not written anywhere in their future.

Native Americans

A minority indeed, Native Americans are very poorly represented in research settings. Perhaps more recently a larger number of students have enrolled in college and are graduating. Native Americans are perceived by others as being shy, introverted and not very communicative. Since they rarely establish eye contact, some individuals consider them untrustworthy. They are typically soft-spoken and tend to establish dialog among themselves, rather than with others whom they do not know. However, they retain a very strong connection with the Earth and are extremely perceptive of their environment.

A more dedicated effort should be made to try to incorporate Native Americans into the workforce to generate a truly diverse environment. Extremely tight family ties also exert pressure on students who have joined colleges far from their residences, and who could be perceived by their communities as outsiders.

There is a constant battle in the mind of minority individuals who struggle to follow their passions, but find their loved ones judging them unfavorably because of it.

Mentoring Minorities in the Classical Setting

Mentoring programs established in centers, academia or industry should be sensitive to the issues that minorities face. Since it is the ultimate goal of an interdisciplinary research program to have the best mentored individuals, it is critical to start cultivating good mentoring practices at each institution. It is therefore not advisable to generate groups that are exclusively formed by minority students, since then the diversity will be lost. It is recommended to generate vibrant mentoring programs where diversity is present and discussions do not gravitate exclusively towards the particular issues of some populations. Participants will enjoy listening to and understanding the challenges that different populations are experiencing. In this way, non-minority students will be able to understand others, and in turn minority students will hear, perhaps for the first time, that those whom they have always considered to be privileged also face challenges.

It is thus not advisable to isolate minorities from the mainstream of the organizations to which they belong. In the first place, it sends the wrong message, and it also generates a group of people who already know their reality; and sharing it among themselves does not bring the main issue to the notice of the entire institution.

The same is true for women. Issues with women have been discussed in multiple settings and opportunities and are the focus of consistent elaboration. Generally, though the recipients of the messages are women who are already very much aware of the issues.

It is time that both men and women sit together to prepare agendas and delineate courses of action with the ultimate goal of dissipating the barriers that impose obstacles to women's progress. Following the same principle, minorities and non-minorities should start interacting more, and committees, organizations and groups inside universities, and workplaces should reflect that diversity. Addressing diversity by creating a group of minorities is not the way in which diversity should be dealt with. It is not the way the challenges are going to be tackled and much less solved.

> *Articulating solutions together, which results from discussions of a diverse group, will set the appropriate venue to understand and provide answers to the issues that minorities and non-minorities face.*

Mentoring Minorities In the Interdisciplinary Setting

All the challenges described above under the topic of mentoring minorities in the classical environment are still valid in the interdisciplinary setting. In a classical interdisciplinary setting, it is advisable to have participants of multiple disciplines, and to add to this variety thinkers who approach scientific dilemmas differently. That particular setting attracts people who accept, tolerate and embrace different ideas. Often, these ideas are foreign to their train of thought and their positions towards philosophical questions as simple as the interpretation of the truth. Thinkers who welcome new ideas are typically more open to ethnical diversity.

> *In an ethnically diverse population, positions on research, results, and analysis could be deeply different. The richness of groups of that nature is profound. The appreciation that participants will develop towards their colleagues, and their new ways of interpreting facts, will be lessons that they will treasure forever.*

The I–Mentor, in contrast to the classical mentor, often will not be of the same ethnic background of the mentee. In the classical setting, individuals look for figures with whom they can identify, provided that there are some. In the interdisciplinary situation the I–Mentor will be facing many divergent cultures that will also translate into different interpretations of reality.

The I–Mentor should be a figure who has been coached and trained to be the facilitator and catalyst, who promotes positive interactions that will translate into a final creation from the group.

Cultural sensibility is one component of I–Mentoring that needs to be stressed. I–Mentors should be aware of the challenges some cultures face in interacting with others. Often members who do not speak publicly are perceived as uncooperative. This action, or lack of action, rather, should not be misinterpreted as lack of interest. In turn, it should be understood that for some cultures the norm is to keep quiet and perhaps share thoughts privately with one person.

Similarly, interpreting attitudes or styles exclusively as facts not associated with a given background should be avoided. Instead, it is desirable that differences in backgrounds and styles are polished and blended within the group. I–Mentors should expect that after some time and consisting debriefing, all members will try to communicate in a more harmonious way by softening their trends instead of perpetuating them.

The critical participation of the I–Mentor will help convey the message of understanding but also advising. The I–Mentor will understand the reserved nature of some members and make that clear to the group, by whatever means are available, but participants themselves should also start making efforts to contribute. Members should welcome participation and should provide time and space to make others comfortable in putting their views forward. It is a mutual agreement that will translate in a much richer interaction.

Examples from the opposite side are also valid. For some cultures, communication is very direct, and that may not resonate well with others. Some members may understand that contributions in the form of direct comments or strong opinions come from a cultural background where this is accepted. However, the role of the I–Mentor is to coach or help the individual to understand that their message will be more effective and acceptable to others if it is presented in a more "massaged" way. The situations described above may seem trivial; however, it is never enough when the topic of communication is discussed. Conveying this message clearly to all readers is of paramount importance in concepts of interdisciplinarity.

Topics such as interpretation of the truth or different approaches to scientific issues and analysis and elucidation of data will not be covered in this volume, and the reader is encouraged to study the literature on the topic of "The Science of Team Science" (SciTS).

WHAT THE EXPERTS HAVE TO SAY

Interview with Ms. Christina Bruce, Director Office Workforce Management and Development, National Cancer Institute, National Institutes of Health (NIH), Bethesda, Maryland.

Question 1. Would you mind telling us about your background?
I have been the Director of the Office Workforce Management and Development of the National Cancer Institute (formerly known as Office Workforce Development), for 15 years. We take care of the internships/fellowships, and try to populate the pipeline of talent in administration and sciences. We also manage talent development and leadership development for employees at NCI. The office started as the office of diversity, and was expanded later. Then we acquired human capital and human resource services. Along with the expansion came a change in philosophy and approach from reactive to proactive. That means instead of waiting for individuals to come with complaints, our prerogative was try to avoid conflict by making the environment more inclusive, to decrease the amount of complaints. We started by creating a truly diverse office. The core values of our office are around diversity.

Question 2. You have been chosen to respond about questions related to mentoring minorities and women. Is that a topic you feel confident about covering?
I think so. On a personal level I have been a mentor, and at the professional or operative level, we identify and place students in laboratories and administrative areas and ensure that their experiences are successful. We choose their mentors carefully. We also have a program for NCI called Knowledge Management, which is basically a mentoring program, where we select a group of employees every year and match them with mentors in a relationship that lasts for at least one year, and in many cases much longer. Our office provides support systems and relates to the concept of mentoring in many levels. We have been generating inclusive programs for mentoring.

Question 3. Do you think there are specific challenges in mentoring women and minorities that need to be addressed?

Absolutely. It is one of our goals to diversify the workplace and generate an inclusive environment for women and minorities. It is up to management to rise to that challenge. It is also the responsibility of the mentees who are entering the workforce to work hard on that aspect of inclusiveness. For example, often women and minorities are uncomfortable in asking for what they need. Perhaps they do not feel entitled to it, perhaps they think that they are in such an important place that they do not want to rock the boat, they do not want to ask for too much. Then they avoid asking for what they need. I frequently have to tell them that not only are they entitled, but they should also speak up for themselves. If they need something, they have to let the others know or else they will be ignored. It is critical to empower them so that they can believe in their own values. In many regards, it is a cultural problem. For some cultures, individual needs do not count, and the needs of the group are more important.

Question 4. In many cases when needs are verbalized and addressed, the individuals thrive, and that benefits the organization; is this correct?

Absolutely. The mentors should be appreciative of those characteristics that are receptive to learning, and they should hold the same standards when they mentor minorities and women. Making allowances for cultural differences increases the mentee comfort level and learning, maximizing the process of training as well. Our environment comprises highly educated and highly performing individuals, who may have issues with disability, language, cultural authority, communication and family matters. Mobility problems are accommodated easily, but if someone has a language problem, adaptation is more difficult. We need to be careful about equity in mentoring. Women mentoring women is an example. If I have to mentor a young Hispanic intern I will be pushing her to the top, to demonstrate her potential, perhaps much more than a non-Hispanic intern. It is not conscious. Another example is that of women with children or older parents at home *versus* women with no children. Those two groups are going to organize their work in a very different way.

Question 5. You are in a managerial position, and have probably had to provide special accommodation for individuals with specific needs. Is that seen by others as preferential treatment?

I think that if you are managing well and in a healthy environment you are going to be perceived as fair. Needs are going to be different. Settings should be different to maximize productivity. I believe the needs of the new generation are different; they demand much more and we know by experience that one size does not fit all. I think that one can increase productivity, generating a healthy environment that in turn will increase employee loyalty. Over the years, I have had working mothers who thought that they should leave the work environment and stay home. Instead, I suggested that they take a job share. I know many managers would be very uncomfortable with that, but these women gave 110%, because they felt respected and appreciated.

One of the things I hear from young minorities, on the topic of asking for what you need, is about believing in yourself, and that things will work out. They tend to worry more about what the reality is going to be for them. Their life experiences and what others have told them makes them believe that they are less advantaged than the mainstream.

Some of that is related to their community. As an example, a Native American young lady wanted to go into research. Their elders considered she needed to do clinical training to return to the community to serve it better. Her needs and the needs of her community collided. Native Americans believe that the rule of the brave makes it necessary for young and strong people to stay ahead of the community and pave the road, by providing reassurance that the landscape in front of them is safe to cross. That implies that young individuals who want an education need to return to their communities, because they are permanently and perpetually linked to their origin. Such traditions are deep rooted. For those reasons, and also internal reasons, minorities and women often feel that they are not worthy, and that their needs do not matter.

Question 6. Do you suggest then that the mentor has another very important role, not only professionally but also touching upon those issues that have an impact on the overall performance and training of the individual?
Yes, discussions, positive reinforcement and communicating the role of the person in the overall plan and operation may settle any internal concerns that mentees have.

Question 7. You mentioned the influence of the community for Native Americans, but what about the role of the family in the Hispanics?
Many families fear having a member away and far from them. They believe that having a career, particularly for women, will be limiting in establishing a family. Individuals feel the need to fulfill the expectations of their families, they do not want to disappoint them.

Question 8. Do you have any strategy when it comes to minorities and women to be particularly effective?

I think that mentors need to be aware of obstacles and challenges that individuals face when making the decision to study or take internships or move up the career ladder. An understanding of the cost at which the mentees come to learn and to live far from their families will help communication between mentor and mentee. Mentors do not need to adapt their style, just to be cognizant of the other things that are going on in that person's life. The mentor should be flexible in working with the mentee, and they should work together to find the best way for them to absorb knowledge.

Question 9. Are you suggesting that we need to mentor the mentors?

Absolutely. In our internal mentoring program we have training for the mentors. It is not just knowledge about bringing the person along, it is also about covering communication and cultural issues, to maximize the experience.

Question 10. Is there any change in the traditional practice of mentoring that you would envision to improve its practice for minorities and women?

Something we are trying to implement in our office is to model the new style of peer mentoring that is now prevalent in the private sector. There, peer mentoring is done in a more organic and formalized way. The private sector has pioneered tools and resources. Women bond together on an informal basis, either at a dinner date, or a lunchtime session. They compare and share experiences. Sometimes a senior member of the group will provide the benefit of their experience. That is also the importance of the role model.

Question 11. Would you give some specific advice for the mentors of females and minorities?

Flexibility and engagement are the key elements. It is hard to give advice. People who embark on the journey of mentoring minorities and women are those who are already convinced. It is very hard to ask someone to do this if they do not believe in it. In some ways, we have already crossed that bridge in our program, because we enroll those mentors who seek to participate. It is also important to find out the best way for the mentee to communicate their needs.

Question 12. Could you provide some words of wisdom for the mentees (in this case females and minorities)?

There is an expression that I like and it goes "Leap and the net will appear." The implication here is to believe and trust that things will work out. Trust and go for it, do not miss the opportunities.

Question 13. It there anything else that you would like to add?

I think that we have covered everything.

CHAPTER NOTES AND OBSERVATIONS

In this section, you are welcome to write your notes. You could use the following system, provided that you have some time to dedicate to it.

First, just write, do not worry about processing. Just write the first thing that comes to your mind. Use this space to do it. Extend the writing as much as you want or simply write one sentence, or even perhaps just one word. We will call that section *Brainstorming*.

In the second section, you are invited to reflect. The section will be your space to elaborate more about your brainstorming to organize the thoughts and make sense of them. That second section will be called *Reflection*. Although you can work on that section immediately after you have finished your brainstorming, it is advisable to come back to it later, the next day or even a week or two after the brainstorming took place. Unlike the first section, this second one will call for a more organized style of writing, where the brainstorming ideas crystallize to form concepts that you own, that you generated from yourself. Note that those concepts could align with the reading, or differ from it. It does not matter. Those are the concepts you generated through your own elaboration.

Finally, you can summarize, perhaps with the help of bullet points or short sentences, the most outstanding ideas or concepts from the topic. That section, typically shorter than the former ones will be named *Conclusion*.

I invite you to start with this chapter.

Brainstorming

_____

_____

_____

_____

_____

_____

Reflection

_____

_____

_____

_____

_____

_____

Conclusion

_____

_____

_____

_____

_____

_____

CHAPTER 5

Interdisciplinary Mentoring

An emerging area of research centered on examination of the process by which scientific teams organize, communicate and conduct research is known as the Science of Team Science (SciTS).

Scientific research is changing; interdisciplinary work and collaborative work are the most predominant styles in research today. Since science and research are multidisciplinary and based on a large amount of crosstalk, mentoring should follow that trend. Interdisciplinary mentoring is the mentoring of the future. It is the tool of scientists to produce synergy in groups, and to generate multifocal ideas and complex solutions to complex challenges. This concept will be discussed in detail in this chapter, since it is

Interdisciplinary Mentoring in Science
DOI: http://dx.doi.org/10.1016/B978-0-12-415962-4.00005-9
© 2014 Elsevier Inc.
All rights reserved.

the most novel approach to mentoring today. More specifically "team science" is expected to combine specialized expertise, theoretical approaches, and research methods across disciplinary boundaries, producing high impact science (Börner *et al.*).

OVERVIEW

The processes by which scientific teams organize, communicate, and conduct research is known as the Science of Team Science. This discipline promotes team-based research through empirical examination of the interactions, processes, and elements involved in building successful teams. Increasing attention is placed on the understanding of such interactions, and the promotion and support of teams that would achieve scientific discoveries not attainable by either individual or simply additive efforts. An understanding of the difference between additive efforts and synergy constitutes a critical element of the Team Science. Support for these concepts will be beneficial and essential for the success of the team as a whole, measured by positive relationships and the success of the final contribution.

Team work, however is a relatively modern approach to scientific research, as it is the opposite of independent and individual research, a modality well established in academia. The scientist's ability to participate in successful team collaboration can be stimulated by internal needs or external imposition. Strategies to facilitate such participation should be developed to secure the genuine engagement and critical collaboration of every member.

There are many strategies, from short-term, project-specific approaches to longer-term modalities designed to cultivate an enduring transdisciplinary (TD) orientation over the course of an individual's career development. Ideally, an intended outcome of cross-disciplinary education should start earlier at undergraduate level. Some pilot initiatives offer a programmatic framework and reflective space for established team researchers to review their practice, as well as a group learning environment where they can exchange concepts, methods and experience. Currently there is an informative suite of online team science learning modules that empowers visitors to experience team science concepts and methods.

TEAM SCIENCE APPLIED TO THE BIOMEDICAL SCIENCES

There is an increasing realization that "team science" is needed to tackle and conquer the health problems that are plaguing our society. The perception of individuals making discoveries rather than teams is an anachronism. It is clear for the public as stakeholders that scientific progress in areas of medicine is a team effort. It is still hard, however, to remove the persistent concepts of *silos* or *feuds* established a long time ago in academia. Teams are the future of science, as discovery is an interlaced network of complex concepts. Since scientific reality is defined and understood as an intricate web of reactions, processes and pathways, it becomes clear that the implementation of these concepts cannot be achieved by independent researchers, but rather by real teams with a combined background and tools to engage in the resolution of complex problems.

As an example, solving the obesity epidemic most likely requires the integrated interactions of researchers who study lipid metabolism, genetics, and cell growth; endocrinologists; pediatricians; internists; surgeons; exercise physiologists; nutritionists; behavioral researchers; psychologists; and economists, to name just a few. Academic research institutions, that maintain a classical setting, are not conducive to encourage such diverse teams to coalesce. Collaboration is common; true coordinated teamwork is rare. Effective problem-focused organization across disciplines or departments is far from the norm; training and mentoring with the expectation that the trainee will have a successful career in such a team environment is virtually non-existent. Most often, in academics or industry, the lone inventor/innovator or the multifunded "independent" laboratory head is seen as the pinnacle of success. We are wrong to persist in this single ideal if the goal is to translate scientific discovery into improvements in human health.

Successful multidisciplinary research teams require transformational leadership that is capable of developing a shared vision within the team and sustaining the team over time; infrastructure that is of value to all team members; facile communication based on collaborative education and respect that allows constructive disagreement; and finally, the recognition that the dynamic structure of a team, in and of itself, requires work to sustain.

Transformational leadership describes leaders who are motivators, moderators, and mentors and who have the ability to connect disparate groups.

The importance of the mentoring role of the initial team leader cannot be understated. It should be assumed, during the connective thinking process, that all members may eventually take a role as leader of the group at some time, as new projects are developed with shifting focus. Leadership dedicated to mentoring would facilitate the progression of entry level scientists who are expected to work as a consortium and collaborate productively to move into future leadership positions of their own. Based on this concept, the team will be a dynamic structure that will produce the best trainees as well as the best team scientists.

Transitioning to team science should be perceived as a culture change that requires intensive commitment. Organizations need to identify their transformational leaders and foster multidisciplinary team development with their help. Creating interdisciplinary "cultures" has been a topic on interest to many. In her recent contribution, J.T. Klein introduces a series of strategies, based on activities, interest and leverage on pre-existing resources, that provide critical elements to move forward.

THE INTERDISCIPLINARY MENTORING (I-MENTORING) PILOT INITIATIVE

In any pilot multidisciplinary initiative, the importance of the mentoring role of the initial team leader is critical. It should be assumed, during the connective thinking process, that all members may eventually take a role as leader of the group at some time, as new projects are developed and a shift in focus is implemented.

An interdisciplinary mentor has to be able to:

- sacrifice self-interests;
- control dominant individuals;
- ensure that all members are acknowledged; and
- ensure that projects and resources match the interests and priorities of the team.

Pilot efforts will generate a mentoring culture able to change the way that mentoring has been seen until now. Additionally, the I-Mentor will act as the conduit to help effective connections and stable collaborations.

Based on scientific research on silo settings, mentoring has been traditionally considered a vertical relationship that creates silo thinkers, and independent researchers generally isolated.

This new approach trends to generate open minded mentors that in turn will be the engine behind the success of the scientists involved in team groups.

Pilot experiences should be typically composed of two phases:

- Phase 1: creation of robust mentoring programs in the participant organizations (departments, laboratories, organizations, and institutions).
- Phase 2: training of selected interdisciplinary mentors (I-Mentors) chosen from their respective organizations.

The outcome will be to have robust trained I-Mentors with the ability to return to their mentoring programs and train their members, generating additional I-Mentors and eventually, I-Mentees.

The existence of I-Mentors is critical to the development of the collaborative units that are central to interdisciplinary science (I-Science). Having a mentor with the ability to understand the core of the concept of I-Science will assist in the overall wellbeing of the team and the generation of ideas in an environment of freedom, respect and trust.

DEVELOPMENT

Phase 1: Creation of Robust Mentoring Programs in the Participating Organizations

This phase encompasses the support of the creation or enhancement of pre-existing mentoring systems in each organization. The concept is to develop strong programs able to generate I-Mentors and I-Mentees on the second phase. Each participating group should assign a representative to receive training on how to set up a successful mentoring program. The diverse nature of the collaborative group is of critical importance for the outcome.

Phase 2: Training of Selected Mentors (I-Mentors) Provided by the Respective Organizations

Phase 2 constitutes the core of the collaborative unit. Training I-Mentors is a novel activity that encompasses numerous steps and aspects. The training will seek to produce a solid I-Mentor who:

- will understand the concept of I-Science;
- will exercise self-reflection;
- will learn to be open minded;
- will exercise respect and trust;
- will be able to put their own interests to one side;
- will look for common ground;
- will be able to see the whole picture;
- will be generous;
- will be a potential leader if circumstances demand it;
- should have enough plasticity to occupy diverse roles in the group and jump from role to role as needed.

Since these competencies are not acquired immediately but rather are part of a conscious change in mind set that requires a process, it is expected that the participants receiving training will take part in periodic refresher sessions that will bring the concepts discussed during the training back to their minds.

It is expected that the I-Mentors, once trained, will involve themselves in interdisciplinary research, and will be prepared to take the interdisciplinary group to the next level of thinking and achievement.

Training based on initial deep self-reflection is proposed. It will then be followed up by an intense set of exercises seeking tolerance and adaptability. Since I-Science gravitates around collaboration and diversity of background and opinion, tolerance is paramount. Similarly, the search of common ground is a desirable skill to develop and master.

I-Mentors should be capable of distancing themselves from the problem adopting common ground that will facilitate connections and processes of discovery.

Although the diverse nature of the team should persist, I-Mentors have to remember that the success of a group is dependent on all the team members. Traditional mentorship has been focused on individuals, their development and career progress, as well as their personal wellbeing. I-Mentors should metamorphose that concept without losing sight of their objective: the group. Hence, if traditional mentoring called for individual success, I-Mentoring calls for group success. Traditional mentoring takes place, generally, from a supervisor closely related to the discipline of the mentee. I-Mentors on the other hand, could provide trans-disciplinary mentoring, by focusing on the success of the team and including the mentee as one part of the team. The establishment of the mentor—mentee relationship was often imposed by educational structure and the academic program requirements or obligations. I-Mentors should be available to all the individuals in the team, regardless of their hierarchy or position, being consistent with the idea that the discipline is not as important as the message conveyed by the I-Mentor. It is desirable that I-Mentors focus on the outcome of the team.

Peer mentoring becomes even more relevant in the setting of interdisciplinary mentoring. I-Mentors should crosstalk and generate vibrant ideas, challenged by others on a frame of respect or trust. I-Mentors would be those able to analyze, think and revise ideas without feeling challenged or scared about their personal success or funding.

OUTCOME

The outcome of these experiences should provide the basis to generate teams committed to solve complex problems, with a multi-disciplinary approach, where the focus of the group is the team effort rather than the independent approaches.

Teams should be led by I-Mentors trained specifically for this purpose and selected from the team's participating organizations.

A true collaboration should be evident not only when the members involved are able to reach consensus, but when the team reaches the stage of thinking as one.

HYPOTHETICAL EXAMPLE

A step-by-step example of the I-Mentoring approach will illustrate the concept much better. Remember that this is just an example and that the concept could be applied to multiple settings with diverse structure as far as the desired outcome is interdisciplinary research.

The topic of obesity, as mentioned before, constitutes a clear case of interdisciplinary research in which a multiplicity of disciplines and an array of expertise and backgrounds are required. A successful outcome can only be achieved when the complexity of the problem is understood by a wide-ranging group of experts. Not only are different specialties required, but also diverse ways of looking at facts and outcomes.

In a complex topic such as obesity, groups as diverse as basic researchers studying lipid metabolism, genetics, and cell growth; endocrinologists; pediatricians; internists; surgeons; exercise physiologists; nutritionists; behavioral researchers; psychologists; members of the community; counselors; parenting specialists; economists; and probably others should be recruited. First, form a consortium of thinkers to try to understand and define the problem to establish strategies on how to solve it. Next, use the following strategies to implement the I-Mentoring process:

1. Recruit groups with desired expertise cited above.
2. Select an I-Mentor for each group.
3. Meetings with I-Mentors should be held periodically to train them as a group.
4. I-Mentors return to their groups and start working inside their groups to initiate the members in the new interdisciplinary interactions.
5. Once this step is achieved, the I-Mentors should decide when it is time for the groups to meet together and start synergizing and evolving their thoughts as one.

All these steps take time. However, the outcome is worth the effort.

In our hypothetical example, it is envisioned that each participant group, reunited by different methods in a large team (step 1) selects one I-Mentor (step 2). This is a very delicate and time consuming event, since the future and outcome of the large interdisciplinary team largely depends on the interactions of the I-Mentors with the participants in the groups and the interactions among the I-Mentors in the team. The I-Mentor does not need to be an expert in the topic, or the more senior individual on the team, or the leader of the group. The I-Mentor needs to demonstrate the capacity to think about others, be able to listen and understand, and be a consensus builder. It is not desirable that the expert or leader in the field takes this role, because it is very hard to disagree with a leader who is an authority and expert in the field. It is very difficult for some individuals (particularly from Hispanic or Asian backgrounds) to verbalize difference of opinions to a higher authority. That is why the selection of the I-Mentor constitutes a critical step for the groups and a decisive factor in the outcome of the team.

Once the I-Mentors have been trained (see more about resources at the end of this chapter), a good sense of camaraderie should have been built, and the relationship among the members should have intensified. It is desirable that I-Mentors interact and have at least a few meetings to discuss science or the question that the final team is going to address, in this case the obesity epidemic. Even when the I-Mentors are not experts, these initial conversations are crucial in setting the tone and the dynamics of the team in the future.

I-Mentors are now ready to return to their groups and train mentees and possibly new I-Mentors. Simultaneously, each group will be strengthened by the presence of the I-Mentor, who represents a unifying figure and a reference point to address questions and tensions.

Each individual group will work independently in addressing issues of concern, at the same time as they will work together with other groups as part of a team. It is desirable that meetings held by the team have the presence of the I-Mentors at all times, since they are crucial to group cohesion.

Let us discuss our example further. Each of the groups will be evaluating different questions and solving different challenges; however, all of them are part of the same team, that as a whole wants to contribute to the big question: the obesity epidemic. Nevertheless, the focus of individual experts may differ. Even the language spoken may differ. It has even been proposed that the interpretation of reality may be different when the background of the individuals participating is diverse. That is what generates an even more challenging and interesting outcome in the world of interdisciplinarity.

Individual groups may start coalescing with the same question in mind, only to later understand that they need to take a step back to facilitate understanding among themselves. A psychologist may not think that there is a genetic factor affecting the accumulation of lipids in the adipocytes of some individuals, while some other members have probably spent years studying multiple approaches to elucidate that exact question. The I-Mentors should be able to put all the opinions, points of view, concepts, and dogmas on the table and look for consensus, establishing pathways for the whole team to be explored. The I-Mentors should be able to persuade their members of the importance of understanding the validity of the questions that other groups have, the focus of other disciplines, and the essence of the collaboration.

I-MENTOR TRAINING

Training I-Mentors is not trivial. It is usual to attribute to mentors qualities that are part of their nature, of their personality and not learned or acquired by training. This is probably largely true. There are some individuals for whom communicating, listening, and caring are normal qualities of their lives; however, for others, those qualities have to be acquired, learned and practiced often to make them a permanent part of their personalities. Being a classical mentor is a good step to become an I-Mentor; however, being a classical mentor may constitute an obstacle to learning new possibilities, views, and aspects of mentoring that uniquely identify the I-Mentor.

I have divided the journey of training I-Mentors into a series of steps.

- Step 1: *introspection*. Each individual has fears, unanswered questions, dilemmas, pending issues, dark thoughts, and more to deal with. It is desirable that these are explored to some extent before starting the training process, or as part of the first step in training. It is not expected that each I–Mentor solves these problems, but it is expected that at least they will be able to face them, acknowledge them, and continue training with this self-knowledge, and how it could interfere with the development of their role in a given group.

- Step 2: *development of flexibility.* A deep analysis of one's psyche may help to bring a different prespective to each I–Mentor in training. These challenges, explored after profound introspection, may bring substrate to elaborate more and more on personality issues. Once that is covered, individuals may need to elaborate on their beliefs and dogmas, and start challenging them. In that way, openness and flexibility of thinking will be initiated and cultivated. This exercise will confer an incredible feeling of peace and connection. That is exactly the type of grounding that is needed to be able to connect to others and to transmit genuine thoughts and feelings.

- Step 3: *active listening.* The I–Mentor by this point acquired two superb qualities, inner connection and flexibility. The acquisition of the ability to challenge their own ideas without fear will make the I–Mentor ready to establish communication with others. Now is when active listening is essential. Active listening is a dynamic way to understand, comprehend and be part of a dialogue, even when the information received contradicts the mentor's own beliefs or does not align directly with their knowledge. Active listening requires an extra effort to absorb and process new information, to be able to motivate mentors to think about it and not negate it.

- Step 4: *communication.* According to recent publications, individuals desiring to work in interdisciplinary research, education and training projects should immerse themselves in the languages, cultures and knowledge of their collaborators (National Academy of Sciences 2004). Not surprisingly, participants in teams who have reached positive outcomes found that understanding "other disciplines," methods, traditions, terminology and underlying assumptions was a facilitator of communication. Communication is often one of the most difficult aspects of relationships; communication in cross-disciplinary teams is even more complex. The role of the I-Mentor is of critical importance here, since the outcome of the team depends directly on the ability of members to communicate, relate to each other, transfer ideas, new concepts, teach, and train. Personal assumptions need to be suppressed, and team members need to understand the assumptions of other disciplines, so that the views of all members can be used to achieve the team's objectives. The I-Mentor could facilitate this by arranging discussions based solely in one or two questions answered by different members. That simple exercise will bring to light the facts that represent assumptions. Group members will start to understand where their colleagues are coming from by understanding the whole position of the discipline they are representing. That does not mean that there is absolute agreement or concurrence on everything; it is just an understanding that there are different interpretations of reality or multiple interpretations of the same fact.

- Step 5: *consensus building*. Probably the most challenging aspect of the I-Mentor role is requiring individuals to be able to combine, accept, and blend opinions coming from diverse backgrounds and different schools of thought. Consensus building should start with a few I-Mentors first, perhaps those with an obvious scientific connection. They in turn can start building consensus with a different set of I-Mentors (who in turn had built consensus among themselves). There is always space to build consensus, and there is always time to build it. The art is to find the conduits, the roads, the different avenues that sometimes are not the most obvious, but back roads that will lead to the desired destination.

Engaging people in a team is another task that requires talent and training. Teams may go through phases of apparent low productivity, or phases that move at a different pace from the one expected by some of the members. It is intrinsic to different sciences to evolve projects or prove hypotheses at their own pace. The time required for some experimentalists could be quite different than the one employed by epidemiologists. Although in a team setting the topic is the same and the energy of the group should gravitate around the central theme, it is natural to have some groups that are more closely engaged and articulate much better and at the same pace. The I-Mentor should also be able to convey this apparent lack of synchronicity to their members so that everybody understands and is prepared to face cycles of productivity alternating with other less productive cycles. The I-Mentor should be a figure who operates in different spaces and times, and who accommodates the needs of individuals to focus all interests.

ONE MORE ROLE FOR THE I-MENTOR

Eigenbrode *et al.* published an article referring to the use of a toolbox in the biosciences. The article, entitled "Employing Philosophical Dialogue in Collaborative Science," proposed the discussion of philosophical questions prior to setting up the team. The authors present the readers with questions formulated with the mindset of generating deep conversations and inducing self examination. By applying this toolbox, the authors aim to achieve identification of the philosophical disparities and commonalities among team members. The questions are formulated individually at first, but are then discussed as a group. Examples of the application of this powerful instrument are described in the article. The discussion is led by a facilitator who cannot take part in the dialog, but rather facilitates it and keeps it in focus. The I-Mentor is equipped to carry that activity, and is already sensitized to look for consensus building components that will be critical to the outcome of the team.

All these expectations placed on one person are a lot to master in a short period of time. We have to understand that the I-Mentor is also biased towards their own discipline and the *modus operandi* and processes that characterize that discipline. However, everyone should be supportive of the I-Mentor role. The I-Mentor should not be the one who applies discipline, acts as a preceptor, gives orders, or corrects individual's behaviors. Rather, the I-Mentor is the person who shows the roads to understanding, who places two or three bricks in the consensus structure, and who offers opinions that, in turn, will promote reflection, discussion, and ultimately agreement; even agreement to disagree.

In many instances the I-Mentor may need to keep quiet when indeed what they really want is to express their opinion. As in classical mentoring, that is not the real role of the mentor.

The properties of the I-Mentor, and the differences from the classical mentor, are summarized in Table 5.1.

As detailed in Table 5.1, I-Mentors need to develop and exercise many characteristics to be able to play the role of a consensus builder among other roles, in a team.

Table 5.1 Properties of I-Mentors and Classical Mentors

Traditional Mentoring	I-Mentoring
Focused on the mentee's development and career as well as their personal wellbeing	Focused on group success
Generally from a supervisor, closely related to the discipline of the mentee	Transdisciplinary mentoring where disciplines are diverse and not necessarily close to the I-Mentor background
The establishment of a mentor—mentee relationship is sometimes imposed by educational structure and academics programs	Relationship established independently of academic obligations
Minimum or no training required	Training required to master skills that are specific to the team setting
No connection with other mentors required	Connection with other I-Mentors required
Style has to adjust to each individual mentee	Style is structured to work in groups, minimum adjustment required

It has been proposed that:

"since the trend in collaborative research seems likely to march on, it is up to those now in training to gain the skills necessary to prosper in research teams" (Thriving in an era of Team Science, Burroughs Wellcome Fund).

However the means to reach that goal are far from being implemented. This book pursues the concept of I-Mentoring as one tool and instrument to achieve training, knowledge, and real understanding and preparation of the emerging scientist to face the challenges presented by the science of the future.

OBSTACLES

General

It is inevitable that the I-Mentor will find obstacles. As with individual mentees, there may be communication difficulties, or a perceived lack of interest or enthusiasm by the mentee. In my many experiences of talking to mentors, those two situations are the most common elements of interference with the mentoring relationship. The mentees, on the other hand, find disturbing the lack of time with the mentor, and highlighted their inability to communicate candidly about frustrations or lack of engagement with their activities (studying, dissertation, fellowship, and work). These obstacles will also be present within groups, and will be one of the factors that I-Mentors will need to transfer to the individual group mentors; the I-Mentor deals with challenges emerging from the team, and not from individuals. This particular situation can be hard for team members and group mentors to understand, and sometimes, because the nature of the individuals operating as I-Mentors, it can be difficult for I-Mentors as well.

Communication

Singled out as the most common challenge in human relations, communication is the central topic that I-Mentors have to master and implement from the very first day, no matter how clearly the statements about communication have been established, and how common the issue is for everyone. The fact that communication can be understood differently by different people is not an excuse.

In the multidisciplinary example outlined previously, the obesity epidemic, understanding different "research cultures" does not happen spontaneously, even when everyone is committed to the task. Understanding other cultures comes after listening, asking questions, understanding the answers, engaging in active dialogs, and participating in common thinking. For that to happen, two main components are needed: the speaker and the listener. The former has to be sure that they can transfer knowledge in a way that is understood, not just communicated verbally, but transferred actively in such a way that listeners coming from different research cultures and expertise are able to understand and assimilate the central concepts. Many individuals are not equipped to do that; they do not find value in collaborations with others who do not speak the same language or those who need basic explanations of their disciplines in order to be able to join the group. That silo mentality has been engrained in our minds for so many decades that we embrace it to the point of considering that if we have to explain the "abc" of a science to somebody, that somebody will not be able to contribute to our knowledge or understanding of the problem or the question we are trying to solve. Many people do not see a problem with that, but new science does. New science looks for the collective intelligence as the ultimate goal, with a different reality and a convergent concept of knowledge and truth.

Reality can be perceived as a combination of ideas, as an opportunity to blend concepts that were conceived to be together. The reality is no longer what is proven in a test tube, isolated from the social aspect, or divorced from the stakeholder opinion or the quantum physics conception. As difficult as this concept may seem, it has to be explored and embraced, to help the believer to grow as a person.

I-Mentors may have the important task of communicating concepts of that nature, at the same time as reiterating to the group that no one reality is more accurate than another. The reality they are looking for together will be reached as a team, and not as individuals. Communicating that message to the team, as well as improving communication among members, is critical for the operation of the group. Only when individual members embrace that concept in their minds will they be ready to communicate, as well as being open to communication. This dual role, wrongly defined as active—passive, is as difficult as it is ambiguous. Typically, a good communicator would rather speak than listen, and opposite to that, some people would rather listen than speak or communicate. This ambiguous role of being active listener as well as active communicator has to be developed, and training in it is also desirable. Everyone should be able to be an active communicator; although if not born with that quality, they can improve their abilities with practice. Silo scientists learn that communicating their research, by publishing, attending conferences, and giving talks, is central to their careers. Now, they have to learn to appreciate other sciences and improve their skills in speaking to others in a language that is understood, inviting dialogue rather than intimidating. In addition, they need to open their minds to practice active listening and engage in discussions and challenges proposed by other scientific disciplines. Adopting this transformational state is paramount for the success of the team.

> *Communication, then, has to be exercised from the inception of the group to ensure the establishment of a cordial and collegial atmosphere that invites participation and generates synergy.*

Commitment

Similarly to classical mentoring, commitment is essential to the positive outcome of the relationship. In a multidisciplinary setting, it is even more challenging to engage everybody and to ensure that all of the participants are working together. Commitment is strongly connected to communication. The more the group talks, the more they understand each other, accept their differences, embrace their cultures, and participate actively. Commitment depends on the interest that the members have developed on the topic and the engagement they have with the team. The I-Mentor should be able to sense the level of engagement of the members, understanding that it is going to fluctuate. At times some members will feel closer and will make alliances, perhaps because of their matching jargons, similarities in their cultures, or simply because they "click". Ups and downs are going to be observed and as a facilitator, the I-Mentor has to understand that their role is to make the group realize that they are going through a phase. The I-Mentor has to facilitate the search for a reason and hence a solution.

Feedback

One of the most difficult aspects of mentoring is the proper delivery of feedback. In classical mentoring, it is advisable that the mentor—mentee pair discuss in advance the format and setting that each prefers to deliver and receive feedback. Although in reality the message is going to be the same, the environment and/or the conduit matters. Most young mentees may choose an electronic format for delivery of "bad news," and perhaps face-to-face for good news. For the classical mentor, face-to-face is probably the most favored method of feedback delivery. In either case, positive or negative criticism, face-to-face should be the method of choice. The mentor should carefully read the gestures and body language of the mentee in order to adjust their words to achieve the appropriate language and tone. It is very well known in communication that both members of the pair who are trying to establish a dialog will tend to adopt a defensive attitude that is not conducive to understanding or even listening to the feedback. I have listed some steps that may alleviate the obstacles created by feedback delivery:

- Determine format: electronic (e-mail, text, computer letter), telephone, face-to-face (if so go to the next point).
- Determine setting to deliver feedback (work place, residence, park, restaurant, corridor, outside the office, other).
- Establish frequency of delivery: in a serial fashion or each time it is needed (for instance, once a month or when a report is reviewed, when a lecture is presented, or when a paper is written).
- Agree on which style both members of the pair feel comfortable with. Direct speech, soften, indirect, thorough questioning, inductive.
- Confirm that both members are comfortable with the agreement, and also that the agreement can be changed according to the experience and the maturity of the relationship.

It should be noted that although apparently premature, there is no better way to approach this challenge than to face it before it is a challenge. It should be noted also that mentors are not the only ones delivering feedback, and mentees are not the only ones receiving it. One of the benefits for the mentors in the mentor—mentee relationship is precisely mastering the art of providing feedback. When this is established for the mentor—mentee relationship, it becomes a competency for life, and is a valuable one to have. Often, mentors do not have time or the style to polish their speech, and are too direct with the mentee when providing criticism that could hurt or simply not be welcomed. If that is the case, mentors should understand that the single most important thing in this relationship is the ability to provide feedback that should not only be satisfying for the speaker, but captured and understood by the listener. Urgencies in the delivery of feedback often do not assist the outcome. Mentors should be able to transmit an idea or an observation with the strength needed to reach the mentee, but with the tone and style appreciated and valued by the mentee as well. When this happens, mentor and mentee will be conducting a dialog.

FEEDBACK ABOUT FEEDBACK

Although it may sound strange, the mentor—mentee pair should have feedback about the feedback. After a period of time, they should revisit how this component of their relationship is working for both, and in both cases.

If that simple intervention was taken into account in other relationships, many problems in life and in the world in general would be avoided!

Active Questions

Asking questions, a model chosen by many psychotherapists, is probably the most effective way to provide feedback; however it requires extreme patience and ability by the person delivering, and great openness and positive predisposition by the receiver. Sometimes, the receiver is not able to see the issue at stake and there is no question that will be able to make him/her open the eyes and realize what the point is. Asking effective questions is an art that should also be exercised more often in multiple settings. Once it is acquired it will stick. Some examples may help to clarify the active questioning style.

Elizabeth, a senior postdoctoral fellow, had just delivered a talk at her department in a prestigious university on the East Coast. Her mentor decided to offer her some feedback about it. They met in the mentor's office in a closed door type of setting. The mentor started the conversation by indicating that the presentation went well. Immediately afterwards, however, he indicated that the mentee did not handle the questions properly. He continued his argument, contending that the way in which Elizabeth considered the questions before giving answers did not make her look serious. He went further in saying that handling questions in this way reflected badly on her, and made it seem that she was not knowledgable about the topic. Elizabeth left the room feeling very demoralized. After that conversation she felt bad, and her attitude was more towards a defensive than a reasoning one. The dialog made her negate almost everything that was said to her, instead of making her reflect.

How many things could have been done differently? How many different scenarios can you delineate for this simple one-to-one round of feedback? The answer is: many. Take a couple of minutes and reflect about your style if you are a mentor, and how would you have delivered this piece of feedback to your mentee in a simple situation like the one described. Reflect about *attitude*. Elaborate about *setting*. Give a thought about *outcome*. If you are a mentee, think of how you could have distanced yourself from the message (depersonalizing it), and used it to extract something positive from it. Think of ways in which the message could be modulated to be used in the future. Own the criticism, and brainstorm on how to avoid this challenge the next time. Talk to your mentor about the setting for feedback delivery, re-define styles and try to make them understand that favorable outcomes will be much more possible if feedback is presented in a different way.

The same situation could be run through the method of active questioning. Even in a setting as the one described, that could result intimidating for many, the mentor could have approached the mentee in a different way. Active questioning examples are shown below:

- What do you think about your talk yesterday?
- How do you feel?
- How do you feel about the questions?
- Why do you think you hesitated to answer question "x"?
- Why do you think you went in circles when Dr. Brian asked you about "y"?
- Is there anything we can work on to give you more confidence about your knowledge and how to deliver it?
- Is that something you think you can work on? Do you see any value on doing that? Are you willing to put the effort?
- Do you think that in the future you need to practice questions and answers before giving a talk?
- Do you think this type of feedback is positive for your future?
- Would you consider this exercise important for your next job interview, for instance?
- Do you understand that handling questions properly makes you look more professional?
- Do you think that answering questions using a different style could improve credibility?

If feedback is presented as an active exercise using some of the questions listed above, the mentee has to acquire a pro-active role to be able to reply, and the final product is achieved not just through a speech imparted by the mentor/supervisor, but rather through a concept elaborated by the mentee with an active reflection component guided by the formulation of questions.

Exercising this type of feedback delivery is recommended for a variety of situations, and once the pair get used to this dynamic, the effect will be perceived immediately, the dialog will flow much easily and feedback delivery will be a less painful process.

Additional tips to improve feedback delivery:

- Be sure to agree on setting.
- Establish the best time for both members.
- Confirm that pre-established date and time are still the best for both members.
- Do not agree on a time and date if you or the other party are pressed by time.
- Be prepared for a flexible time commitment. A 30 minute meeting can get into a longer conversation you do not want to miss or postpone.
- Be open minded to deliver and to receive.
- Although this is personal, do not take it personally. Be objective.
- Do not try to find arguments to reply, rather focus on listening.
- Try to put yourself in the other person's situation, especially if you are delivering feedback.
- Arrange for a post-feedback meeting whenever you are ready to discuss some of the issues. Never do it at that time. You need time to regroup.

Feedback In the Interdisciplinary Setting

We have covered the topic of feedback in general, and we now need to explore in more detail how people will adjust to have an I-Mentor who, in addition to their individual mentors, will be delivering feedback. If establishing agreement between two individuals was complex, being able to communicate and present feedback to a group is much more challenging. However the I-Mentor will focus their feedback topics on the operation of the group as a whole. It is advisable that the group meets frequently to reassess performance and to elaborate on ways to improve situations or to avoid conflict.

The I-Mentor should participate in these meetings, and should understand the scientific culture of the individuals taking part of the group and their different approaches. However, the group as a whole has to develop as a new entity, with new dynamics intrinsic to the organization; group dynamics that will change according to the phase of the group. I-Mentor interventions will be probably more frequent and needed at the beginning, when the team is a fresh working structure. In the more stable phase, when differences are understood and accepted, the role of the I-Mentor will decrease, to gain momentum later when the original goal that brought the group together is achieved and the structure is reaching the end. This part is really critical, and the role of the I-Mentor is of paramount importance to help the team coalesce as one thinking unit, acquire collective intelligence, and come up with the answer as a unique entity, without a predominant school of thought, but rather with a novel approach to understand and visualize a challenge. At this decisive stage of the group, the I-Mentor plays their most important role. By then, the I-Mentor will have matured with the team, and will have learned multiple skills inherent to the demographics and dynamics of the team. The team has reached its goal, and the I-Mentor needs to guide them to coalesce and reach a conclusion that originally united them all.

DATA ANALYSIS AND INTERPRETATION

In multidisciplinary teams, the collection of data is enhanced by the collaboration of multiple groups that, individually, produce their results in form of quantitative or qualitative data, depending on the discipline. Collecting data is not a challenge. The challenge is their interpretation, connection, and agreement. Members of the team should be aware of the fact that some approaches, if designed for different purposes, can produce sets of data with conflicting interpretation.

In a multidisciplinary team put together to study the obesity epidemic, multiple disciplines will participate actively in a search for recommendations, based on data analysis to help understand the depth and complexity of the subject. It is very important to establish a goal and to define a vision right at the beginning of the establishment of the group, with the understanding that both will evolve during the development of the team's activities. Since each independent group will operate with different strategies to approach their area of study and to solve their questions, the times and expectations of each component will differ. An example following the topic of our hypothetical team will serve to illustrate those points.

In the obesity study team, a group of basic science researchers could be focusing on genes that are involved in the accumulation of fat on the cells and others that fail to remove fat from cells. They might compare the behavior of different metabolic routes that operate in non-obese individuals and how these may differ in obese individuals.

Epidemiologists may want to look for longitudinal data on cohorts composed by individuals that have been normalized for age and other factors such as smoking or socio-economic background and ethnicity.

Social workers may consider interviewing individuals and visiting their households to collect data that produce information regarding habits, family composition, structure and relations.

Psychologists may want to have interviews and collect information regarding behavioral aspects of the members selected for the study.

While collecting data from the analysis of the basic researchers will be quantitative, the responses to the approaches of the sociologists and psychologists may be qualitative. Epidemiologists on the other hand, may want to start applying models that will function with the kind of historical data they have collected.

> *What language is the group going to use to explain their results to each other? What areas of synergy will develop? What approaches are going to be implemented to find areas of overlap? What explanations are going to be explored to understand conflictive results?*

Since disciplines are becoming narrower and focus is more specific, every day scientists find more challenges in communicating to each other. It seems that jargon has invaded our lexicon, and we cannot explain our findings in terms that other scientist can understand, much less lay people. In an interdisciplinary setting, a universal language must be spoken. Scientists have to make an effort to understand each other and they have to be able to explain their thoughts in a clear manner. If needed, a tutorial course on terms and approaches could be offered to try to increase the knowledge of those who are not specialists on that particular topic. Although that approach could be natural for some, it might be a waste of time for others. That is typically the attitude of those who feel superior and that claim that their discipline is more important than the others. In a way, it is like saying that everyone should speak my language, even when I am in a foreign country. This is a very important message to those choosing their partners in multidisciplinary collaborations. Perhaps the most talented scientist or clinician, or the behavioral scientist who wrote 20 volumes on a topic, are not necessarily the best collaborators. Conversely, those with a predisposition to learn, share and understand will be the best partners and will work hard to make the goal of the group happen.

A senior researcher on chemical carcinogenesis commented on how difficult it was to engage epidemiologists on his research project. I had the chance to ask him how he solved the challenge. He indicated that he spent six months taking a course on epidemiology to be able to understand his colleagues the epidemiologists. Then he tried to establish a dialog and engage his collaborators in his own topics of interest. He was ultimately able to establish collaborations that crystallized in relevant publications. The scientist, however, expressed his frustration about the difficulties he experienced when trying to explain simple assays developed in his laboratory to measure and quantify DNA damage. This experience seems to indicate that some individuals with a large capacity to learn and who are willing to communicate will go the extra mile to achieve their goal. Others with a more arrogant attitude, on the other hand, will never move from their comfort zone to capture concepts foreign to their everyday reality. This is a lesson to keep in mind when trying to approach collaborators.

If these challenges are overcome, and communication among different disciplines is finally achieved, a new emerging challenge to be faced is that of the interpretation of the data. Since opinions are going to vary, it is desirable to agree on a method for doing this before the process starts. It is advisable to have a subgroup of individuals able to combine the multifocal approaches and assemble a meaningful set of conclusions. Being ready and prepared to support conclusions that are not aligned with the initial hypothesis is one of the possibilities that team members have to ponder.

Interpretation of the Data

Let's revisit once more the hypothetical case regarding the team conclusion phase.

The analysis of the data emerging from the different disciplines involved will cover areas from molecular biology to behavioral science. The instruments used to obtain those results differ widely, from a genetically engineered mouse to a questionnaire. Valid and valuable results are obtained from both sources, but combining and relating their significance can be a hard task to accomplish. Molecular biologists may conclude that interaction between two genes and the impact on a signal transduction pathway play a critical role in obesity. Behavioral scientists may conclude that patterns of behavior associated with obesity are identifiable, and could be the target of intervention. How may those two very different approaches be aligned? Is there an area of congruency or at least some tangential sector among those two positions? Perhaps the I-Mentor could be the one favoring the brainstorming of those two groups in order to achieve a conclusion that encompasses both results. The I-Mentor should be facilitating dialog and integrating ideas and positions that may initially look irreconcilable, but which can be amalgamated into much bigger concepts. The I-Mentor should ask the groups to reflect on their understanding of the definition of obesity, and be sure everybody on the team agrees on it. It would not be unreasonable to think that for a basic scientist, obesity is the condition in which metabolic pathways are involved, for a clinician, the definition could hinge on clinical signs such as weight, cardiac condition, and diabetes, while for others, the condition could simply be a matter of individual perception, a subjective situation, than a list of signs or pathologies. Defining the entity or the issue under study seems trivial, but it is not. It is essential to solve discrepancies and to start on the same page. This also helps the group to understand that there are other realities besides the ones they know, that go beyond a test tube or a survey.

AIM FOR THIS

From the many authors who cover the topic of mentoring, Johnson and Ridley (2008) were able to compile most of the traits that, in my opinion, a mentor should have. I will list them here, and recommend you to read *The Elements of Mentoring* by these authors. I have highlighted instances in which classical mentoring and I-Mentoring differ, or are not quite similar.

Johnson and Ridley advise that one should practice the following:

- Select your protégés carefully (note that I personally avoid using the term "protégé" because of the connotation of inferiority).
- Be there.
- Know your protégé.

- Expect excellence (and nothing less). In the case of the I-Mentor, expect and encourage the team to think as one (and nothing less).
- Affirm, affirm, affirm and then affirm some more.
- Provide sponsorship. For the I-Mentor, the role of advisor would be more appropriate than that of sponsor.
- Be a teacher and a coach.
- Encourage and support.
- Shape behavior using reinforcement. The case should be made here regarding the interpretation of "behavior," since that is quite different in the classical individual mentoring experience compared with the I-Mentoring experience. Behavior towards the jelling of the group and the amalgam among disciplines should be reinforced constantly, in order to obtain a well constructed team.
- Offer counseling in difficult times.
- Protect when necessary. The I-Mentor should be cautious and understand than their role is to protect the group, and not specific individuals. That could be rather counterproductive for the articulation of the group.
- Stimulate growth with challenging assignments. Rather stimulate growth by challenging individuals to be open minded and stressing the importance of operating as a unit, rather than as a collection of individuals.
- Give protégés exposure and promote their visibility.
- Nurture creativity.
- Provide correction, even when painful.
- Give the inside scoop.
- Narrate growth and development. In the case of I-Mentoring, the narration should refer to the progress of the group as such, rather than individual progress.

- Self-disclose when appropriate. I-Mentors are also learners, and they are part of the group. As such, their experiences, challenges and doubts should be part of the interactions among members of the group.
- Accept increasing friendship and mutuality. In the case of the I-Mentor, friendship with individual members of the group and not others should be avoided. Rather, the I-Mentor should balance their relationship and befriend the team as a whole, if applicable.
- Teach faceting.
- Be an intentional model. The I-Mentor should be a model in multiple directions, not only as an integral person but also as a person that integrates.
- Display dependability.

WHAT THE EXPERTS HAVE TO SAY

Interview with Dr. James Gentile, President Research Corporation for Science Advancement, Tucson, Arizona.

Question 1. Would you mind telling us about your background?

When I was born, I was very, very young...

I have a background on genetics mutagenesis and biochemistry. I was the Chair of a department in Hope College for 30 years. I was also the President of the Environmental Mutagen Society, and the international society, Research Corporation, a 100-year-old organization committed to fund high risk/high impact research.

Question 2. What type of work do you do and for how long have you being doing it?

I graduated and immediately got myself involved in science. I have been involved in science for around 40 years, teaching students for 30 years, with nine years in corporation research, funding interdisciplinary research, the science of the future. Now I am going back to Hope College to use educational systems to build the future scientist.

Question 3. You have been chosen to respond about questions related to interdisciplinarity. Is that a topic you feel confident about covering?

Yes.

Question 4. Do you think there are specific challenges in the topic of interdisciplinary mentoring that need to be addressed?

Yes, many. I tried to address collaborative issues by creating a program called "Scialogs" (from science and dialog). With that program, discussions on solar energy, and emphasis in nanotechnology have been supported. Highly qualified individuals are invited to participate and get funded for their ideas, on condition that they come to a meeting in the Biosphere II, in the Gordon Conference style. An isolated atmosphere facilitates interactions, and meetings are extremely focused. The idea behind this was to generate more interactions that will crystallize in a funded collaboration. We offer participants a sum of money if they come up with an idea. The project has to be explained on the last day in a time frame of five minutes. Pay attention to this: they are telling their new idea to competitors. What blew my mind was that in that environment of competition, when somebody presented their idea and asked for questions, the collaborative framework was developed by other individuals responding: "that is a great idea, but you could add this and that to make it even better." That was a real collaboration being born. The second time, more and more collaboration ideas came up.

Social workers have studied the interactions of this experience. The interdisciplinarity, though, gets challenged by authorship issues. The first author is often recognized as the one who did the work, the last one is frequently a senior scientist, perhaps a Nobel laureate. The people in between are technicians or less senior scientists. Arranging the order of the authors among three equal collaborators is in conflict with the classical academic reward system. The editors are not synchronized with the Science of Team Science (SciTS). Journals have to change, have to adapt, to recognize talent in a different way. A different approach should be in place to provide more support for interdisciplinarity.

I am going to apply some changes in Hope College. I will probably generate workshops in tune with the Scialogs. There are around $38.7 billion from private funding to support this kind of initiative. I will be meeting with scientists at the Howard Hughes Medical Institute (HHMI) to have a discussion on this particular topic. How do we fund this type of science? How do we support these talented investigators and move forward this kind of science? In the future, we hope to visit the White House to discuss federal monies and how we will articulate the practice of funding.

Leaders have to lead, and ask for changes that will overcome these challenges.

An interesting study on collaborations run at the Poly pedal lab in Berkeley by Bob Full, showed that teams constituted by only engineers failed, all-male teams failed, all-female teams failed, and teams comprising only African American members failed. A really diverse team is the one that succeeds.

Ethnic diversity, gender balance and complex specialties combined will contribute the most. Heavy dialog, constant communication, and crediting people for their contributions are critical components of success.

The most complex questions in science will only be solved by the right teams.

Question 5. Do you think that the private sector will be pioneering these efforts?

Most probably the private sector will be contributing the initial money to move projects and ideas championed by interdisciplinary teams. Federal monies, on the other hand, are still going to be funding more traditional and classical styles or research. Little by little, these patterns may switch. The private sector will set the framework for others. Riskier projects funded by private money are very different from those funded by public money. The difference is protecting the money provided by tax payers.

Question 6. Do you have any strategy when it comes to interdisciplinary mentoring to be particularly effective?

There are many mentoring levels: students, teachers, developing new faculty, and career progression. Senior advisors provide mentoring that has to be systemic to be effective. Intentionality of educators and advisors will take time to be built. I was very intentional on where my trainees went to do their postgraduate work. I cared a lot about where they went. Choosing what was right for them, rather than the most renowned professor, was critical for their success. Human beings are more important than fame of places, or fame of persons. That constitutes mentoring at different levels.

Question 7. Is there any change in the traditional practice of mentoring that you would envisage to improve the practice in the setting of interdisciplinary mentoring?

I was working at the interface of genetics and biochemistry in the early 1970s. My advisor asked me to consult with a second advisor with expertise in genetics. Mentoring was not as common then, so it was an innovation to request the University of San Antonio to accept two advisors, given the nature of the project. That in a way was multidisciplinarity. Mentoring is a continuum, and a trust. Dialog should be one of the changes that has to take place in the new type of mentoring you are describing in your book.

Question 8. Would you give some specific advice for interdisciplinary mentors?

No-one can be an interdisciplinary mentor on their own. No-one has knowledge of every discipline. Having multiple mentors, and being open is my first piece of advice. Focus should be place for training people to be able to work with multiple disciplines, without feeling the need to know about every discipline. Nobody is superior, no science is more important than any other science. Scientists will need to overcome the supremacy they have held for many years.

Question 9. Would you provide some words of wisdom for the mentees?

Believe half of what I say, and challenge the rest.

Question 10. Anything else you would like to add?

Lose boundaries, dialogue more.

CHAPTER NOTES AND OBSERVATIONS

In this section, you are welcome to write your notes. You could use the following system, provided that you have some time to dedicate to it.

First, just write, do not worry about processing. Just write the first thing that comes to your mind. Use this space to do it. Extend the writing as much as you want or simply write one sentence, or even perhaps just one word. We will call that section *Brainstorming*.

In the second section, you are invited to reflect. The section will be your space to elaborate more about your brainstorming to organize the thoughts and make sense of them. That second section will be called *Reflection*. Although you can work on that section immediately after you have finished your brainstorming, it is advisable to come back to it later, the next day or even a week or two after the brainstorming took place. Unlike the first section, this second one will call for a more organized style of writing, where the brainstorming ideas crystallize to form concepts that you own, that you generated from yourself. Note that those concepts could align with the reading, or differ from it. It does not matter. Those are the concepts you generated through your own elaboration.

Finally, you can summarize, perhaps with the help of bullet points or short sentences, the most outstanding ideas or concepts from the topic. That section, typically shorter than the former ones will be named *Conclusion*.

I invite you to start with this chapter.

Brainstorming

_____

_____

Reflection

_____

_____

_____

_____

_____

_____

Conclusion

_____

_____

_____

_____

_____

_____

CHAPTER 6

Building a Mentoring Program

HOW TO ORGANIZE A MENTORING GROUP

You are now considering establishing a mentoring program in your organization. To be sure that you are on the right track, I would advise you to follow some principles listed, and elaborated on below.

Sense Genuine Need

In many instances, the organizer of the mentoring group feels a need to start a mentoring program but indeed that reflects their own needs, and not necessarily the needs of the organization. It is very important to sense the real need for the program before starting the effort. This goal could be achieved by speaking to people, and by establishing focus groups or "think tanks" that after an

Interdisciplinary Mentoring in Science
DOI: http://dx.doi.org/10.1016/B978-0-12-415962-4.00006-0
© 2014 Elsevier Inc.
All rights reserved.

elaborated discussion and brainstorming reach the conclusion of establishing a mentoring group. Then, when the genuine need is established, you need to move forward with the effort.

Obtain Permission

Obtaining permission or authorization depends on the organization and the level of command you possess in the organization. No matter how powerful you are, it is critical to make the effort somehow "official" through the appropriate channels. Also, be sure to have a group and not just one person being responsible for the effort. This will encourage sustainability and continuity, and cover for any turnover in the leadership of the group.

Obtain "Buy In"

Obtaining permission is just a bureaucratic step, while obtaining "buy in" is a much more involved task that requires the help of a wide network. Once the genuine need has been assessed, the process of building your attendee list starts. That aspect of the process requires a certain degree of thought. Provided that you follow the previous point, and there is a group behind the organization of this effort, then the network will be larger and diverse. Careful thought should be given to the outreach of the group, since your audience needs to be substantial to reach the objectives established. The group should be diverse in all possible angles of diversity, unless it is a dedicated group, like female engineers for example. Gender, race, and discipline, should be balanced. In many instances, and depending on the setting, it will be challenging to obtain buy-in of certain individuals, but that is your responsibility, your commitment to the initiative. Do not downplay this step, since it is critical for the future of the group. Be sensitive to avoid built-in tensions among members that will not help but rather stress differences. Be aware of preconceptions among departments (in a university setting) or competitors (in a research setting). I would caution here that being extremely aware of pre-existing situations among members could led to a certain degree of paranoia, which will discourage people from participating. Be sure you understand that being aware does not mean excluding, it simply means being aware and discussing with your organizers the fact that some challenges may emerge during the development of the program.

Define and Understand Your Audience

Once your audience is established, you need to find the common denominator. Are those members together because they have the same goals? Is there a common goal that unifies them? Could that "invisible" goal be established after the first meeting? Remember that you had a goal in mind when you were motivated to start a mentoring program. Do not get carried away by your original idea—or the idea of your organizer team—and try to establish at the very beginning what is the goal of your new group. A word about the size of the group is relevant here. It depends on many factors. One of them is funding. If your group involves lectures, books, and materials, the number of participants will be limited by the amount of funding. If, instead you are admitting everybody who wants to participate, limitations will be dictated by the size of the room and the length of the meetings. I would not go higher than 25 individuals. Consider also that there will be a drop-off in the number of members through natural attrition. This does not mean that the group is not effective or well-conceived, it is just the way that groups operate.

Provide Personal Commitment

Building trust is the uppermost important factor. The members need to be there because they trust you and the other organizers, but they will be present in mind and body if they trust each other as well. Building trust is your obligation. You should be there and deliver whatever you promised to deliver. You should provide the means to achieve the goals the group established at the beginning of the program.

Require Personal Commitment

In order to make this group effective, you are entitled to require personal commitment from the stakeholders. Attending sessions, being an active member, listening, being attentive, providing feedback in a positive constructive way, and respecting others, are features that are a must for everyone who considers them-selves a member of the program. A word about confidentiality is timely. In many instances, groups are formed by members of the same department, office, or research team. This generates a great deal of tension, and may prevent people from being sincere and totally open about comments or thoughts. If a commitment to confidentiality is established at every session, these tensions can be alleviated, at least in part. Be aware of these situations, and try to be candid when commenting on them.

Make it Open to Everybody

Although the nature of some groups calls for limited participation, there is an enormous advantage in having the group open to "outsiders." On many occasions, people who are involved in an organization cannot move forward because of "staleness" or redundancies in the way of thinking. It can take just one significant comment from somebody totally foreign to the group to shed light on the interactions, and to generate creative ideas and new ways to seek solutions. Do not ever underestimate the power of questions asked from ignorance. Again, it depends on the goals of the group, but try to be flexible and open about participation. Everyone will benefit from obtaining mentoring, whether facilitators, coaches, or members participating in the discussions.

Look for Alignment with Pre-Existing Organizational Strategies

Depending on the setting in which you are working, some pre-existing strategies of the company, academic unit, or research center may be in place. Care needs to be taken to synergize with these strategies, rather than generating competition or the false perception of replacement by this new effort. Alignment with the organization is essential to obtain buy-in of members who do not want to participate in initiatives that can be labeled as "second-class."

Reassess Often

Your flexibility is paramount. A group can change its initial goals at regular intervals. Reassessing goals and the means to reach those goals is critical to the life of the group. New objectives, and dynamic goals can surface every time people meet and talk. Consider that some sudden change in management take place, or that a grant is cancelled, or funding terminated. Reassessing the goals of the group from long term to short term should be allowed, and priorities should be re-considered often. The fact that you as the mentor demonstrate flexibility also calls for a reciprocal action from the participants.

Establish Metrics

Perhaps one of the most difficult steps to take while designing your program is the method by which you will measure the effectiveness of the intervention. In some cases, this may be established by the group, perhaps not at the beginning of the sessions but once the dynamics have been put in place and the group is consolidated. There are other cases where the organization requires evidence of success by deliverables, or surveys from existing participants. That is very specific for each organization, and is outside the scope of this book. However, organizers should be aware that these metrics may or may not reflect the real outcome of the group. Since it is very difficult to measure personal growth or transformation, the parameters to be evaluated should be the closest to those events, with all the caveats involved on those concepts.

Avoid

Whining Sessions

It is not unusual to witness a lot of whining in some mentoring group programs. It is what people use as an outlet or escape valve, to be listened to and to vent. Although in a way that is "healthy," try to avoid generating a perception that your program is just that, a place to sit and complain. Your program is a place for transformation and growth. Only on rare occasions are these milestones going to be reached by whining, but rather by finding the positive and building on it. Be attentive and listen, be sure the facilitator allows some complaining, but transform the concepts into something positive; this will allow the group to grow and thrive.

Personal Agendas

It does not escape those who have participated in more than one meeting that there are individuals who bring a personal agenda to the table, and they will not leave until that agenda is fulfilled. They want you to listen to their issues, attend to their needs, and solve their problems. Often, these are irrelevant to the issues for the group and represent their personal interests. Most of the time, such agendas are hidden until you suddenly realize where the individual is coming from. Selfish and self-centered people tend to do this. Those individuals also tend to boycott the group if the group does not revolve around their interests. They may also leave the program because they are upset about it and will criticize it. There is nothing you can do with such people. Just be aware, and perhaps address the issue with the group if such a situation has taken place under your watch.

Dominant Voices (Thieves of Time)

Very common among scientists are those individuals who like to listen to their own voices. It could very well be that such a person will be one of the members of your group. These individuals tend to intimidate others, stealing their space and time. Conversely, they rarely pay attention to other group members, and active listening is not one of their skills. But there is hope. The facilitator of the group should be sensitive to the situation and be able to help this person evolve and grow, by cultivating patience, generating strategies on mastering active listening, and practicing silence exercises to build skills that will improve their careers and life in general.

Drainers of Energy

For some unknown reason there are some individuals who have a great capacity to drain the energy of a group. In general they are demanding, not as the "thieves of time" just described, but through their moaning and pessimism. Members of a group should have high levels of energy, and be active and engaged.

Individuals who drain energy accomplish this by taking a long time to process their thoughts or to verbalize concepts, and they are always objecting to proposals or finding negative aspects to ideas. People go home exhausted and with the sense of not having accomplished anything after listening to such negative individuals. Unlike the people with personal agendas, who will eventually leave the group, the energy drainers will remain, as they find this is the outlet they need to verbalize their frustrations. It is useless to try to counteract those individuals with potential solutions to their eternal negativity, because they will always find something to complain about in the new ideas they are offered. Rather, the facilitator should limit the attention given to these members, and try to focus on leveraging the energy of the other members. Do not allow the vampires to hijack your energy! Remember, the group is at risk.

REMEMBER THAT YOU ARE DEALING WITH SCIENTISTS

It is worth reflecting on the characteristics of scientists. Although there are multiple exceptions to the rule, in general you will be facing individuals who are pragmatic, who relate to results, who express themselves in a detached way, and who judge others easily. Also, for some of them, expressing feelings is a skill they need to build, and if a meeting or conversation is getting very personal, they will retract. Scientists are used to making conclusions; their whole career, and in part their lives, revolve around conclusions. Typically, such conclusions are reached after looking at data, so it will not be unusual for scientists to keep asking the facilitator for evidence, numerical proof, or facts that support an idea that is brought up and is being discussed. Scientists are skeptical by nature.

They will question every hypothesis (mainly if it is not theirs), they will oppose every notion, especially if it is a new concept that shakes their comfort zone. Remember, scientists are very smart people who keep thinking all the time, and they are very hard to convince about new possibilities. They need to learn how to build flexibility into their minds, mainly when it comes to personal development. Keep this in mind. On the other hand, they are learners by definition and they will learn fast, once their barriers are dropped and trust is built in the group. Once that milestone is achieved, you will find wonderful souls ready to support and help each other in the quest for human transformation. Once they are there, they are there to stay, they will become disseminators, the ones who will convince others, who will persuade colleagues and family members that mentoring is a journey for everyone.

> *Facilitate the group to devise solutions, to generate alternatives to grow, to build together, to be ready to move to the next step, and make sure each individual transform himself into a disseminator.*

MENTORING GROUP—*MODUS OPERANDI*

Although there are no written rules on how to run a mentoring group, there are some basic activities that you should consider using to enhance the interactions and to achieve the goals established.

Check-In

This simple activity will help set the tone for the session and will bring individuals from their external environment to the group space. The activity must be monitored to prevent hijacking the time allotted to it. One minute per person will take 20−25 minutes of the entire session, and the same could happen in the check-out. Although both activities are essential, they have to be limited. One example of a question frequently formulated by facilitators at check-in would be "What are your expectations for today?", or "What is your state of mind?" It helps the facilitator to understand the type of mood the audience is on that day at that particular moment. A trained facilitator will be able to conduct activities according to the state of the group, or return frequently to the topic, to re-assess. Check-in is a very important activity because it levels everyone. All the members have to participate, and there is also the benefit that the activity helps people to find out more about each other every time.

Check-Out

Similar to the check-in, the check-out activity is important to give closure to the session and to bring individuals to reflect and conclude about the experience of that day. Both activities help re-group, center, and be aware. It helps to check-out with a question that requires a short answer; an example could be: "sum up in one word how you feel now." Some of the answers to that question could be: energized, empathetic, confused, frustrated, enthusiastic, expectant, or flexible). It is possible that by the time of check-out, some people who were reluctant to respond at check-in are now ready to participate. Activities practiced during the session, exchanges maintained, and active listening practiced during the time preceding the activity may have exerted a positive effect on some members, loosening them up and encouraging them to talk freely. For some, check-out is a more relaxing time than check-in.

Invited Speakers

As a facilitator, your role is to fulfill the needs and goals of the group by providing activities that will support and guide members towards their objective. It must be understood that changes do not happen overnight, and that new concepts need time to gel and be part of the person. Ideas may need to be offered more than once, and in different ways. Keep in mind that different speakers may be able to reach different members, depending on style, dynamic, and background. Be sensitive to the issue that you are working with scientists, so that a speaker with a certified degree would be more credible. Additionally, be mindful that for some, a uniform (such as a military one) carries a lot of respect, while for others it may generate detachment. If the same concept (i.e. leadership) is presented more than once in different ways, the chances of making a wider impact are greatly increased.

Panels

A good option to reach out to different styles in one session, and overcome the issue mentioned above, is the organization of a panel, with the objective of answering a question or developing a topic. The facilitator has to be extremely sharp to sense who would be the best panelist to invite, not only because of their expertise (that ideally has to be diverse), but also because of their style and ability to influence all members of your audience.

Discussions

Once your group is consolidated, honest conversations can be handled, and perhaps these are necessary from time to time, not only to sense everyone's opinions, but also gauge the interactions. For some, "aha" moments only take place while brainstorming to elaborate an answer, so dialogs are essential to provide those opportunities. Conduits to reveal insights are precious, because insights are self-realizations that will stay with us forever, even without executing them every day. A trained facilitator will be alert to those moments, whether or not the person actually reveals them. Maturation of the group by insights is a desirable outcome for any mentoring group.

Books

No matter how much a concept is verbalized, for some members of the group, ideas, strategies, concepts, or methods have to be written down to be evaluated, absorbed and understood. In such situations, the inclusion of one or more sessions devoted to analysis of a book can be critical. Be sure that the book is practical, short and to the point, so everybody has time to read it and digest it—remember that you are dealing with scientists! For some, it will be a unique opportunity to understand concepts, for others less so. However, there are instances where books provide ideas that can be revisited as the book is re-read. That cannot happen with discussions or panels.

Individual Coaching

Although quite costly, some mentoring programs provide individual coaching. This is probably much more so with companies than in academic settings, but if you have funding and need to think about wise ways to spend it, individual coaching will certainly be one of them. For some members it will be very useful, for others less so, but everyone should have the opportunity to experience the activity and to be sure that coaching is or is not for them. Selecting appropriate coaches for scientists is not an easy task. Most "life coaches" are trained on programs geared towards corporations, businesses, or companies, and do not necessarily address specific issues that pertain to the scientific career. The expectations of participants should therefore be assessed at the start, and it is preferable for them to be low, rather than too high.

Pairing

If funding is not available and interest in providing coaching prevails, pairing participants with mentors could be an alternative. This approach will not replace the function of a coach because of lack of expertise in the area of coaching, but will provide useful advice and experience, beside organizational memory and knowledge about the institution. Pairing rules should be determined by the pair and not by the facilitator, since the relationship will be evolving as the mentor—mentee relationship. Facilitators should be aware that the fact that the program offers pairing does not limit the program to a mentor-match style of intervention. That perception should be avoided.

New and Group-Generated Activities

As an indicator of a highly mature group, activities that emerge from the group itself represent the success of the facilitator in consolidating the group and generating buy-in and presence from the participants. Facilitators should be open to such creative activity, and should promote its inclusion in the program. Activities of this sort are variable, ranging from an outdoor gathering (typically the outdoors is a catalyst for dialog and mind opening) to a particular speaker, movie, video, course, or workshop that the group considers essential for their development. A volunteer experience is a great opportunity for the group to improve their cohesiveness.

Specific Skill-Building Activities

There will be cases in which the facilitator schedules activities specifically oriented to build a skill, to provide concepts about a particular topic they consider essential for the development of individuals in the group. Such activities vary from group to group and from facilitator to facilitator. It is advisable to adopt such activities as you go along, and to adapt them, if possible, to the needs of an evolving group. Such topics might include networking, establishing effective collaborations, presence, active listening, learning how to provide feedback, learning how to receive feedback, managerial skills, organizational skills, and family and work life balance.

Community Outreach Activities

This concept may sound foreign for many and that is certainly unfortunate. Returning to society is probably one of the things scientists do not consider important or relevant because many of them believe they are giving a lot to society through their research. It is, of course, true that if it was not for scientific research, many of the challenges facing us as a society would not be overcome. However, there is something very relevant about "giving back," and mentoring groups should be aware of this and should embrace it. Outreach activities can take multiple forms. Individuals might volunteer in different places in their communities, and the group as a whole could also select an activity for which they could take responsibility as a team. Giving back is good for both the giver and the recipient, it brings a smile to the face and a lift to the spirit. This is another opportunity for the group to coalesce and generate solid bonding.

Personal Exchange Opportunities

Personal exchange opportunities can potentially expose individuals to other's experiences to which they can relate. Knowing that others may have fear of failure, difficulties with public speaking, anxiety in meeting with their bosses, fear for the future in their careers, or find it impossible to make a decision about the future, can be reassuring. Similarly, understanding that one is not alone in finding happiness in looking at a cell under the microscope, getting excited about discovery, or feeling guilty about spending ten hours in the laboratory when they have a family, can also bring a feeling of relief!

LEARN WHEN TO CLOSE

Although the most difficult time is over now, and people are working together, getting coaching, being able to interact with others, open minded, and ready to share their inside thoughts, termination will eventually come and that will be hard too. Determine when this is going to happen, and remember that your participants are the disseminators. The more they mature, the better mentors they will be, and the message will grow exponentially. It is fine to let go, to be open about new groups coming and new members getting to experience the benefits of mentoring groups. Remember also that the ones leaving the first group can be candidates for pairing, and that the connection among individuals of different groups will be a wonderful opportunity to synergize experiences. Your job is done, although in fact it is *never* done and you will be empowering others all the time, even when you do not realize that you are doing it.

WHAT THE EXPERTS HAVE TO SAY

Interview with Dr. Geraldine Richmond, Noyes Professor of Chemistry, University of Oregon and Chair, COACh program for women scientists and engineers.

Question 1. Would you mind telling us about your background?

I got my undergraduate degree at Kansas State University and then I went on and got my PhD degree at Berkley in physical-chemistry. I was a professor for five years and then I have been teaching at Oregon University since 1985, working in linear optics and spectroscopy.

Question 2. Do you teach at Oregon University?

Yes, some. I teach and I do research.

Question 3. You have been chosen to respond about questions related to the creation of mentoring programs. Is that a topic you feel confident about covering?

It is mostly about personal experience; we are now in the process of developing specific mentoring programs, the COACh workshops and not programs *per se*, but a series of activities focused on mentoring. The programs are designed to give people information that they do not already have.

Question 4. Do you think there are specific challenges in the topic of mentoring that need to be addressed?

Yes I know there are many issues; basically people do not know what mentoring is and so even getting scientists to understand it is very challenging. In our international workshops there is a distinction between what people in the US believe about mentoring, accurate or not, and the non-existence of mentoring in other countries. Not only is there a lack of knowledge on what mentoring is about, but there is no culture for mentoring to develop.

Question 5. Is there any change in the traditional practice of mentoring that you would envisage in order to improve the practice in the setting of modern mentoring?

People need to know what it is. Most scientists do not know or understand what it is. Just informing them about it is an improvement.

Question 6. Would you give some specific advice for those trying to generate mentoring groups?

I think there is a lot of low level mentoring going on, but I do not think we have enough mentoring that really advances the careers of women, to advance their careers in research. Mentoring programs for women are fine, but unless you have higher flyers in the group, the mentoring is not powerful and effective and will keep everybody in the same place. I do not think we do that enough because the high flyers tend to be too busy to participate.

Question 7. Would you provide some words of wisdom for the mentees?

That one mentor is not enough, and that your mentors need to change with your career progression. However, you should have one or two mentors who stay with you for a long time.

Question 8. Would you provide some words of wisdom for the mentors?

Be frank, and if you do not know how to mentor someone in one area, try to help find others who can. Do not try to know it all if you don't.

Question 9. Can you explain what COACh is about?

We started COACh in 1997 because women were not getting the quality of mentoring they needed or the opportunities to advance their careers. In the chemistry field, women were getting stalled. COACh is all about placing women in strategic positions. We generated a series of activities and workshops geared towards women to advance their Science, Technology, Mathematics and Engineering (STEM) careers. The aim was to help women to get to higher positions in their careers and leadership. Workshops would be in negotiating positions at their institutions, and learning effective ways of communication. We have been doing that since 1997 and have now close to 10,000 women who have participated in our activities. More recently, we have had an impact in developing countries as well. We do workshops as well as personal mentoring, and work with institutions to help them change the climate and be more sensitive to women in helping to advance their careers.

Question 10. Do you want to mention any particular situation that was revealing to you in terms of success?

The analysis produced by social scientists who are associated with the program shows that 90% of the participants of the workshops go on to mentor others. They transmit the skills that we teach them. Also, we know that about 90% have indicated that the skills mastered at our workshops reduced their stress level. So, I think those are the two statistics that have really motivated us to keep going.

Question 11. So you have reached much more than those 10,000 women, is that correct?

Oh, yes, the effect is multiplied by many times.

CHAPTER NOTES AND OBSERVATIONS

In this section, you are welcome to write your notes. You could use the following system, provided that you have some time to dedicate to it.

First, just write, do not worry about processing. Just write the first thing that comes to your mind. Use this space to do it. Extend the writing as much as you want or simply write one sentence, or even perhaps just one word. We will call that section *Brainstorming*.

In the second section, you are invited to reflect. The section will be your space to elaborate more about your brainstorming to organize the thoughts and make sense of them. That second section will be called *Reflection*. Although you can work on that section immediately after you have finished your brainstorming, it is advisable to come back to it later, the next day or even a week or two after the brainstorming took place. Unlike the first section, this second one will call for a more organized style of writing, where the brainstorming ideas crystallize to form concepts that you own, that you generated from yourself. Note that those concepts could align with the reading, or differ from it. It does not matter. Those are the concepts you generated through your own elaboration.

Finally, you can summarize, perhaps with the help of bullet points or short sentences, the most outstanding ideas or concepts from the topic. That section, typically shorter than the former ones will be named *Conclusion*.

I invite you to start with this chapter.

Brainstorming

_____

_____

_____

_____

_____

_____

_____

Reflection

_____

_____

_____

_____

_____

_____

Conclusion

_____

_____

_____

_____

_____

CHAPTER 7

The I-Mentoring Program: How to Establish One

BRAINSTORMING

I hope you are reading this chapter after carefully reading of the rest of the book. It is not until then that you will feel able to brainstorm about the value of implementing a mentoring program in your institution.

A WORD OF CAUTION

When referring to mentoring programs in general, the definition should be established. There are many shades when speaking about this and I would like to introduce an informal classification based on outreach.

© 2014 Elsevier Inc.
All rights reserved. 149

OBJECTIVE

As with any project, the need of a goal or objective should be present from the beginning.

- Is your objective to support mentoring at the level of a small group of students, peers, or managers?
- Is your goal to mentor a particular class, a laboratory, or an office?
- Is your objective coming from your needs, or is it a mandate from the leadership of your organization?

All those questions will help reframe the project and the attitude you will take to implement it.

Pilot experiences are in general a good idea, because they help make adjustments to re-think the final product. Of course, each project is different, based on the participants, mentors, and mentees. However, there are generalities that can be applied to multiple scenarios.

WHAT IS A MENTORING GROUP?

The definition is broad. In a general sense, mentoring groups abound, in clubs, churches, temples, hospitals, neighborhoods, schools, working groups, and among friends. Since this book is intended to cover scientific mentoring, I will refer exclusively to that area. I will start with general mentoring in the classical sense, and then focus in the I-Mentoring program.

DO YOU HAVE BUY-IN?

The first element you need to consider having is commitment from others; the buy-in. Generally, this is present when the idea comes from interested people, the recipients, and not from the top.

Once you establish the need for mentoring, either through your own observations or from the group seeking mentoring, half of the work has been done. Having commitment is paramount. Keeping the momentum, though, can be as hard as establishing the initial responsibility from participants.

EXAMPLES OF MENTORING GROUPS

Gathering by Association

In traditional mentoring groups, gathering may start just by association, with a group of individuals who decide to get together weekly, biweekly, or monthly. The objective could be discussion of mentoring topics, invited speakers from outside the group to provide knowledge and expertise, or to allow topics to develop on their own. Reading materials can be disseminated and discussed. This very first level of mentoring requires an organizer (not a mentor, just a facilitator), as the group is mentoring itself in terms of sharing experiences and looking for common situations and the way to solve them.

This approach has the following benefits:

1. Self-organization
2. Simplicity
3. No need of a program
4. No enforcement
5. Started from the bottom
6. Commitment
7. Minimum investment required (in terms of funding from the organization).

However, the results can vary in some circumstances:

1. It is not appropriate to consider that situations that apply to some will be translated to the rest of the members.
2. There is a risk of some participants hijacking the group.
3. Some will use it to whine.
4. Some will use it as group therapy.

If any of those instances occurs, the prime objective of the group will be lost. It is the facilitator (typically the organizer, who sends emails, reminders, gets a room, and brings food) who has to be alert and make sure that all members participate equally. Since there is no obligation to attend, the membership will vary, and that also will be an obstacle to the consolidation of the group.

Enforcing Participation

In a more committed group, enforcement to participate will take the organization to a different level. The outcome of programs that require enforcement will be positive if the commitment or buy-in is there from the beginning. The decision as to whether the group should be static or dynamic (i.e., accepting turn over or new people brought in by others) should be determined as the program progresses. Programs like this will have a facilitator who has a role typically assigned by the organization; attendance should be recorded, and if appropriate, recognition in the form of credits or hours of training should be awarded. Again, there are pros and cons to this structure.

The outcome will be favorable if:

1. Enforcement implies not just participation, but real commitment.

2. The organizer/facilitator is committed as well, and not taking the role just as one more assignment.
3. Participants look forward to this meeting as a way to grow.
4. There are metrics in place defined *a priori* to evaluate the program periodically.

If the perception of participants is that they are under the obligation to attend and do not have need to do so, then the real reason for participation is defeated. The role of the facilitator here is critical, since they must supply the motivation to encourage the members to participate, regardless of the existence of a sign-up sheet.

Evaluation of the effectiveness of the group is very important, and the metrics have to be defined earlier in the formation of the group. One of the reasons why this has to be set up early is because in that way, all of the participants are forced to think about their expectations and combine them to a point at which one expectation is defined. Given that consensus has been built, then metrics to address the expectation(s) are not so difficult to establish. After this, facilitator and participants can meet regularly and periodically assess their operations through short discussions or evaluations at the end of their meetings. The objective can be revisited and reframed according to the progress of the group.

Matching Programs

In this type of programs, the mentee is almost passive and the mentor is assigned to them to try to match certain preferences expressed by the mentee, either in written or verbal form. These programs are common in academia, and also as a part of scientific societies that serve as bridges in the reunion of mentor—mentees. Societies typically build databases with various degrees of complexity where they store information about both mentor and mentee. On occasions, both are asked to fill in forms detailing interests and other demographic data that could be used by facilitators to match the individuals.

These programs have proven useful when the mentee is looking for an answer to a specific question (how can I move to industry? Do I need to do a second post-doctoral internship? Can I change laboratories?). Sometimes, these associations may evolve into solid mentor—mentee relationships; however, they are helpful for specific situations.

Supported Matching Programs

This type of program is applicable to small organizations, typically a group that is part of a large scientific society. The mentor—mentee connection is established by one person, as in the typical matching program, but the facilitator who helps bridge the relationship does so after having an interview with the mentee-seeking mentors. It is a more involved procedure that in general helps establish relationships that are more successful and longer lasting. A mentoring breakfast where four or five mentees sit with a facilitator for 45—60 min and discuss together the basics of mentoring and their individual needs is a good example. The mentees will be asked to complete a questionnaire with their profiles to help the facilitator find a match. After the matching takes place, the mentor—mentee association will be their sole responsibility. Progress in the relationship will depend on the interest and commitment of both the mentor and mentee.

As previously defined, mentoring programs are tools, conduits, or venues to facilitate the reunion of mentors and mentees. Ultimate ownership of the mentor—mentee relationship is the sole responsibility of the members of the relationship, independent of the program that brought them together.

THE I-MENTORING PROGRAM

The I-Mentoring program is based on many of the characteristics of the classical mentoring program. However, it is desirable that those who wish to continue mentoring interdisciplinary groups should obtain extra training.

Taking the interdisciplinary group as a unit, the I-Mentor will serve as the reference person who supports the group as a whole, but does not mentor individually. As such, it is expected that each member of the group should have their own mentor, and share an I-Mentor for the group. The role of this mentor at times overlaps with that of the organizer, the representative, the chief, and the leader.

One of the possible scenarios in the process of I-Mentoring is represented in Fig. 7.1A by five separate groups (large grey circles) with three members each (small white circles). Each member has his own mentor (small black circle). Members of those groups will align in a more consolidated unit (ABCDE, bottom right). When these groups start to collaborate, they will coalesce, and will become one group; this sequence is indicated by arrows. The ultimate goal is to generate a group in which the original boundaries are invisible (ABCDE, bottom left). The fate of the mentors (small black circles) is similar; they parallel the distribution of the individual mentors and mentees at the top of the figure, to become a single entity when the group consolidates (ABCDE and white circle bottom right). Hence, at the time of merger, the I-Mentor will be only one and is the one who moves the group forward.

Figure 7.1B, on the other hand, describes a different scenario. In this schematic the five original groups are already structured as such, and instead of individuals, the large grey circles represent groups (A—E), each one with an I-Mentor. They will coalesce as the arrow indicates (towards the right) and then merge (bottom

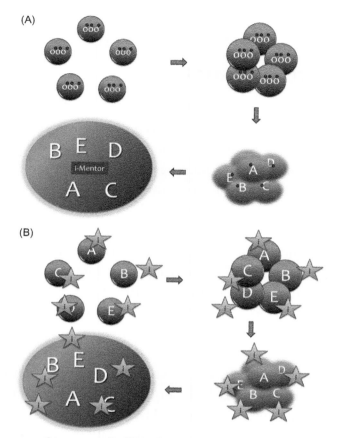

(A)

(B)

Outcome: a community of diverse scientists unified by mentoring connections, ready to establish collaborations and to work on an interdisciplinary fashion

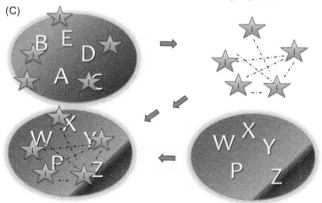

(C)

Outcome: a community of I-Mentors interconnected even beyond the existence of the collaborative unit. These webs of mentors should be able to move into a new group and establish I-mentoring for new units.

Figure 7.1 (A–C) Scenarios in the I-Mentoring process.

right). When the group coalesces completely, the boundaries disappear (bottom left), but the I-Mentors (stars) continue to be part of the group. They will have a close relationship, they will be training together, and may become experts in I-Mentoring who will continue to form a network even if the group dissolves. As such, their training and expertise will determine their ability to become the I-Mentors of a different group (Fig. 7.1C, diagonal arrows). The most important role of the I-Mentor is to understand that now the goal is to support the group, that the group is one entity now, and not the original independent units.

Although it is understood that the I-Mentor in Fig. 7.1A has their origin as one of the individual mentors of the units, both mentor and mentee should be able to look for a compromise in which their relationship can continue at the same time that the new role of the mentor as an I-Mentor is developed. This transition could be delicate at times, but it is in the best interest of the new group that the I-Mentor originates from one of the seeding groups forming the new team, rather than being a completely new character.

> *The original groups of the newly formed team should not feel relegated because the I-Mentor does not come from their group. The I-Mentor represents the interests of the whole team, and not of the original group to which their mentees belonged.*

Table 5.1, as discussed previously, lists some of the differences between traditional mentoring and I-Mentoring.

The first contrast comes from the focus of the mentor, which is the mentee in the traditional mentoring, and the group in I-Mentoring. The origin of the mentoring is typically close to the mentee discipline or unit of study, which is the laboratory in traditional mentoring. However, by definition, in an interdisciplinary team, the I-Mentor is likely to be familiar with one of the disciplines in the team, but not all of them. The establishment of the classical mentor—mentee relationship often originates at the academic institution or organization to which both belong. By contrast, the I-Mentor originates as a seed in an evolving team seeking direction.

For more detailed elements on how to train an I-Mentor, please refer to Chapter 5.

CHAPTER NOTES AND OBSERVATIONS

In this section, you are welcome to write your notes. You could use the following system, provided that you have some time to dedicate to it.

First, just write, do not worry about processing. Just write the first thing that comes to your mind. Use this space to do it. Extend the writing as much as you want or simply write one sentence, or even perhaps just one word. We will call that section *Brainstorming*.

In the second section, you are invited to reflect. The section will be your space to elaborate more about your brainstorming to organize the thoughts and make sense of them. That second section will be called *Reflection*. Although you can work on that section immediately after you have finished your brainstorming, it is advisable to come back to it later, the next day or even a week or two after the brainstorming took place. Unlike the first section, this second one will call for a more organized style of writing, where the brainstorming ideas crystallize to form concepts that you own, that you generated from yourself. Note that those concepts could align with the reading, or differ from it. It does not matter. Those are the concepts you generated through your own elaboration.

Finally, you can summarize, perhaps with the help of bullet points or short sentences, the most outstanding ideas or concepts from the topic. That section, typically shorter than the former ones will be named *Conclusion*.

I invite you to start with this chapter.

Brainstorming

_____

_____

_____

_____

_____

_____

_____

Reflection

_____

_____

_____

_____

_____

_____

Conclusion

_____

_____

_____

_____

_____

_____

_____

CHAPTER 8

In Closing: Mentoring and Synchronicity

Although the constitution of a group and the presence of an I-Mentor are critical for the success of the endeavor, there is one final factor that needs to appear, to encourage individuals to sustain achievement.

I would like to elaborate here on the concept of synchronicity. The term was introduced back in the 1920s by Carl Jung, who was very interested in these phenomena and was able to crystallize the concept many years later in a book called *Synchronicity: An Acausal Connecting Principle*. According to Jung the term refers to *the experience* of two or more *events* that are apparently *causally unrelated* or unlikely to occur together by chance, yet are

Interdisciplinary Mentoring in Science
DOI: http://dx.doi.org/10.1016/B978-0-12-415962-4.00008-4

© 2014 Elsevier Inc.
All rights reserved.

experienced as occurring together in a *meaningful* manner. He also introduced the concept of "archetypes," defined as *inherited potentials which are actualized when they enter consciousness as images or manifest in behavior on interaction with the outside world*. Jung and many followers illustrated these concepts with multiple examples that were published and now are icons of the theory of synchronicity. The classical one being the one described by Jung:

"A young woman I was treating had, at a critical moment, a dream in which she was given a golden scarab. While she was telling me about this dream, I sat with my back to one closed window. Suddenly I heard a noise behind me, like a gentle tapping. I turned around and saw a flying insect knocking against the window-pane from the outside. I opened the window and caught the creature in the air as it flew in. It was the nearest analogy to a golden scarab one finds in our latitudes, a scarabaeid beetle, the common rose-chafer which, contrary to its usual habits had evidently felt the urge to get into a dark room at this particular moment. I must admit that nothing like it ever happened to me before or since."

An additional important concept introduced by Jung was that of "collective unconscious." Jung distinguished the collective unconscious from the "personal unconscious," in that the personal unconscious is "a personal reservoir of experience unique to each individual, while the collective unconscious collects and organizes those personal experiences in a similar way with each member of a particular species."

All the concepts related to those described before have been criticized mainly for the lack of supporting scientific data to validate them. More recently and after the acceptance of the quantum mechanics theory, a series of thinkers and scientists from different fields started to elaborate on new concepts that seem to act as a modern form of these ideas.

MORPHIC FIELDS AND MORPHIC RESONANCE

Let us explore the thoughts of scientist Rupert Sheldrake:

"My hypothesis is that societies have social and cultural morphic fields which embrace and organize all that resides within them. Although comprised of thousands and thousands of individual human beings, the society can function and respond as a unified whole via the characteristics of its morphic field. To visualize this, it is helpful to remember that fields by their very nature are both within and around the things to which they refer. A magnetic field is both within a magnet and around it; a gravitational field is both within the earth and around it. Field theories thus take us beyond the traditional rigid definition of 'inside' and 'outside'."

Basically, Sheldrake and Jung are defining a supra-organization with different names. For Jung, the collective unconscious unifies or connects individuals at the psychological level on the basis of memory. For Sheldrake, the connection is similar but goes beyond the psychological level to involve the whole nature. Sheldrake defines this continuum as "morpho-genic fields" and introduces the concept of "morphic resonance" as the influence of "like upon like." The existence of a connection among similar fields implies that the field's structure has a cumulative memory, based on what has happened to the species in the past. This idea applies not only to living organisms but also to protein molecules, crystals, and even to atoms.

THE PRACTICE OF MENTORING UNDER THE SCOPE OF MORPHIC RESONANCE

Although this could sound like a stretch, there is nothing more refreshing than expanding the mind. So I invite you to take this approach with an open frame of mind, and reflect about the possibilities that this new consideration could bring to you, your mentees and your teams.

Without defining a team or an interdisciplinary organization, Novak described the experience of being part of a team as follows:

"When a collection of individuals first jells as a team, truly begins to react as a five-headed or eleven-headed unit rather than as an aggregate of 5 or 11 individuals, you can almost hear the click: a new kind of reality comes into existence at a new level of human development... For those who have participated in a team that has known the click of communality, the experience is unforgettable, like that of having attained, for a while at least, a higher level of existence" (Novak, 1976).

The description bears an incredible parallelism with Jung's collective unconscious and Sheldrake's morphic fields. Groups that are organized to achieve a goal, in the biosciences or elsewhere, would be connected truly, only when the "click" of Novak, the collective unconscious of Jung, or the morphic resonance of Sheldrake take place.

According to Valerie Hunt:

"...certainly a profitable dialogue could take place between scientists and mystics—perhaps difficult at first, but oh, so fruitful. Both would learn: the mystic to ask more incisive questions and to more carefully articulate and explain deep wisdoms; and the scientists to loosen their mental constraints about the nature of reality to explore 'impossible' ideas. It is my impression that this is indeed happening. Mystically-inclined young people are now entering scientific disciplines whereas in the past they typically chose the arts and philosophy. Some scientists are already performing research with mystics, and several medical clinics have practicing mystics on staff. Scientists and other professionals are meditating, practicing tai chi or yoga, and not just to offset stress but to help them access 'intuitive knowing.' At a recent research meeting, I was struck with the realization that the pioneer thinkers resembled the descriptions of the scientist—priests of the past in their wisdom and personal commitments" (Hunt, 1996).

Since there is no mechanism yet defined or described on how to reach those stages, and improve the performance of the group, I will introduce here some concepts that may be helpful in conquering that level and in acquiring the abilities to understand synchronicity and play along with it.

I-Mentors then, should be able to:

- Recognize synchronicity and quantum leaps. Kuhn recognizes that "now we can begin to accept the fact that basic truths do not stem from information accumulated over the centuries. Fundamental change is not evolutionary but revolutionary: and it occurs in conceptual leaps" (Kuhn and Hacking, 2012).
- Embrace synchronicity. Other forms of communication that do not apply to typical or traditional forms or conceptions could still be valid. As Sheldrake explains in *The Sense of Being Stared At*: "Once again, telepathy would not be an alternative to other forms of communication and to memory, but would work with them. For example it is one thing to see or hear what another member of the group is doing; it is another to interpret this information and respond appropriately."
- Allow yourself to accept that there is an external component. Fields that are no longer connected to a substance but instead to behaviors and thoughts have been classified by Rupert Sheldrake as "morphogenic fields." He believes that fields that

have existed as a result of human lives still exist, and have molded past events as they color what happens today. Furthermore, Sheldrake maintains that when a certain number of individuals of a particular species learn something, it seems to possibly influence, and facilitate, the learning of all other individuals of that species. In *Infinite Mind*, Valerie Hunt supports the idea that the reality of the world lies in fields that interact with each other in dynamic chaos patterns, generating a higher level of complexity. Others, for example Eddington and Schroedinger, contend that science is not dealing with the world itself, but with the shadows of an imaginary world.

- Relax and let go of extreme positions and dogmas. Acceptance of other possible routes of communication, does not mean adherence. An open and receptive mind does not imply observance. Strogatz (2003) refers to intuitive knowledge quite eloquently: "...A handful of mathematicians knew about chaos for 70 years but almost no one else could decipher their jargon or understand their abstractions, so their ideas had little impact outside their small priesthood. And that is typical of the obstacles facing the development of any crossdisciplinary science. Most scientists work comfortably in their narrow specialties, walled off from their intellectual neighbors by barriers of language, taste, and scientific culture."

THE ROLE OF THE I-MENTOR UNDER THE INFLUENCE OF MORPHIC RESONANCE

As an I-Mentor, your role goes beyond participation and observation of the group. As an I-Mentor of a consolidated group, you should be able to recognize synchronicity and help others to approach solutions and answers using the synchronicity built within the group. The I-Mentor should work to produce situations where the "click" takes place, recognize them and be sure to dwell on them, since those will be the most productive moments for the group. The I-Mentor should be trained to induce, recognize and profit by those moments. According to Sheldrake, learning patterns are stored in the morphic fields, and once an activity has been attained it is easier for others to learn it. If groups are contributing with their operations to achieve more successful interactions, this in the end will generate more and more of those successful moments for other groups. Opportunities will arise in which interdisciplinary thinkers will jell and a collective thought will be shared by most. Those events will make the group's moving forward into a reality; they will consolidate connections, open the vision of many participants and generate a sense of maturity and growth. The I-Mentor will treat this occasion as one that is critical for the achievement of the goals, and one that needs to happen often for the complete success of the team.

The Kaleidoscope Effect

The kaleidoscope was invented by Scottish scientist Sir David Brewster in 1816, and patented by him two years later. David Brewster named his invention after the Greek words *kalos,* or beautiful, *eidos*, or form, and *scopos*, or watcher. A combination of those words would mean something close to "looking at beautiful forms," which is a very accurate name.

Sir David Brewster (1781—1868), a child prodigy, built a telescope at the age of ten. He entered the University of Edinburgh at the age of 12, and focused his studies on optics and the physics of light.

Based on a simple principle of reflections of reflections, this amusing instrument is able to generate "ooohs" and "aaahs" from everyone who looks through the little hole. The concept behind this creation is the images produced by particles on a dark background when reflected in mirrors placed at 60 degree angles. Typically, that is achieved by three rectangular mirrors forming the sides of a columnar triangle.

If the magic of the invention is set aside, we are left with a bunch of colorful particles, symmetrically arranged. However, this is where the fascination of the kaleidoscope effect lies.

Translated to the idea of interdisciplinary science, the kaleidoscope effect can be applied to the conceptual blending that collaboration and transdisciplinarity aim to accomplish. The individual components of the kaleidoscopic image are changing all the time, through the movement generated by the observer.

However, all of the reflections are able to conjugate to form an incredible image. Isolated, they will be simple figures, but associated, they constitute an amazingly complex picture that we observe with pleasant surprise.

One image gives place to the next one, and this one to the next. It is this continuum of transformation, this chain of colorful images, that sets the stage for harmony and beauty.

Looking at the kaleidoscope images invites us to think of working in a team of teams, as if each component represents one independent team and each particle one individual. Conceptually, this is a very close representation of interdisciplinary interactions. Multiple arrangements, combinations, and orders can be generated, all of them eye catching and effectively created. Similarly, the transformation of each individual component, formed by just a few particles, leads to a whole generation of new arrangements; it is a simple yet effective system.

Think about your team and interactions. Look through a kaleidoscope from time to time and allow yourself to be amused, to be surprised, to "oooh" and "aaah" freely, and to let the concept of crosstalk and transdisciplinarity germinate in your mind.

Want to persuade your team? Want to engage the individual (particles) that work with you in a positive collaborating environment? Consider building your own kaleidoscope. Consider bringing the concept to the hands and eyes of your colleagues by engaging them in the construction of a simple kaleidoscope with their own hands and as a team effort.

Simple, yet amusing, the task will bring people together and will represent a symbol of the team effort. And that will be just one component. Looking for the other components will come later, and will be a logical consequence of your group working as such.

Looking for collaborations that enhance your unit will be the next step in the conceptual blending.

Here are some easy steps to build your own tool to interdisciplinarity while amusing yourself:

1. Begin by cutting mirror cards into three strips of 4.3 cm wide and 21 cm long. Once cut, tape the three sides together to form a triangular prism with the shiniest sides facing inwards. Push into a kitchen roll tube, so that the prism is flush at one end.

2. Cut two discs of plastic with a diameter of 5.3 cm. One disc needs to be totally transparent whilst the other needs to be frosted. Put the transparent disc inside the tube at the end of the prism. Tape it into place. Pour small, shiny beads into the end of the tube.

3. Place the frosted plastic disc onto the end and secure in place with tape. Turn the kaleidoscope over. At this end, you need to tape a disc of cardboard (5.3 cm diameter) with a peephole cut into the center.

4. Decorate the tube in any way you want, perhaps with the name of the team.

BIBLIOGRAPHY

EMOTIONAL INTELLIGENCE

Bradberry, T., Greaves, J., 2005. The Emotional Intelligence Quick Book: Everything You Need to Know to Put Your EQ to Work. Simon & Schuster, New York.

Goleman, D., 2000. Working with Emotional Intelligence. Bantam, New York.

Goleman, D., 2007. Social Intelligence: The New Science of Human Relationships. Bantam, New York, NY.

Kroeger, O., Thuesen, J.M., Rutledge, H., 2002. Type Talk at Work: How 16 Personality Types Determine Your Success on the Job. Dell, New York.

EMPOWERMENT AND PERSONAL GROWTH

Clance, P.R., Imes, S.A., 1978. The impostor phenomenon in high achieving women: dynamics and therapeutic intervention. Psychotherapy Theory Res. Pract. 15, 241–246.

Jamison, K., 2004. The Nibble Theory and the Kernel of Power: A Book about Leadership, Self-Empowerment, and Personal Growth, Revised Edition. Paulist Press, New Jersey.

Young, V., 2011. The Secret Thoughts of Successful Women: Why Capable People Suffer from the Impostor Syndrome and How to Thrive in Spite of It. Crown Business, New York.

GRATITUDE AND POSITIVITY

Bolles, R.N., 2012. What Color Is Your Parachute? Ten Speed Press, New York.

Emmons, R.A., 2008. Thanks!: How Practicing Gratitude Can Make You Happier. Houghton Mifflin, New York.

Fredrickson, B., 2009. Positivity: Groundbreaking Research Reveals how to Embrace the Hidden Strength of Positive Emotions, Overcome Negativity, and Thrive. Crown, New York.

MENTORING

Adviser, Teacher, Role Model, Friend: On Being a Mentor to Students in Science and Engineering. Washington, DC: National Academy, 1997.

Ammerman, C., Tseng, V., 2011. Maximizing Mentoring, a Guide for Building Strong Relationships. William T. Grant Foundation, New York.

Demi, 1997. One Grain of Rice: A Mathematical Folktale. Scholastics, New York.

Johnson, W.B., Ridley, R., 2008. The Elements of Mentoring, Revised Edition. Palgrave Macmillan, New York.

Hersey, P., Blanchard, K.H., 1977. Management of Organizational Behavior, 3rd Edition — Utilizing Human Resources. Prentice Hall, New Jersey.

Patwell, B., Seashore, E.W., 2006. Triple Impact Coaching: Use-of-Self in the Coaching Process. Bingham House, Columbia, MD.

Stoddard, D.A., Tamasy, R., 2003. The Heart of Mentoring: Ten Proven Principles for Developing People to Their Fullest Potential. NavPress, Colorado Springs.

To Recruit and Advance: Women Students and Faculty in Science and Engineering, 2006. National Academies, Washington, DC.

Wadsworth, E.M., 2002. Giving Much/Gaining More: Mentoring for Success. Purdue UP, West Lafayette, IN.

Wright, W.C., 2004. Mentoring: The Promise of Relational Leadership. Paternoster, Bletchley.

Zander, R.S., Zander, B., 2000. The Art of Possibility. Harvard Business School, Boston, MA.

SCIENCE OF TEAM SCIENCE

Bennett, L.M., Gadlin, H., Levine-Finley, S., 2010. Collaboration and Team Science: A Field Guide. NIH Publication No 10-7660, Bethesda, MD.

Börner, K., Contractor, N., Falk-Krzesinski, H.J., et al., 2010. A multi-level systems perspective for the science of team science. Sci. Transl. Med. 2 (49), 24.

Burroughs wellcome fund thriving in an era of team science. <http://www.bwfund.org/pages/634/FOCUS—Thriving-in-an-Era-of-Team-Science/.

Disis, M.L., Slattery, J.T., 2010. The road we must take: multidisciplinary team science. Sci. Transl. Med. 2 (22), 22—29.

Eigenbrode, D.S., O'Rourke, M., Wulfhorst, J.D., et al. Employing philosophical dialogue in collaborative science. BioScience 57, 55–64.

Falk-Krzesinski, H.J., Börner, K., Contractor, N., et al., 2010. Advancing the science of team science. Clin. Transl. Sci. 3 (5), 263–266.

Jones, B.F., Wuchty, S., Uzzi, B., 2008. Multi-university research teams: shifting impact, geography, and stratification in science. Science 322, 1259–1262.

Klein, J.T., 2010. Creating Interdisciplinary Campus Cultures: A Model for Strength and Sustainability. Jossey-Bass/Association of American Colleges and Universities, San Francisco.

National Academy of Sciences, 2004. 10 findings and recommendations. Facilitating Interdisciplinary Research. Washington, DC: National Academies Press.

Pohl, C., 2010. From transdisciplinarity to transdisciplinary research. Transdisciplinary J. Eng. Sci. 1, 74–83.

Whitfield, J., 2008. Group theory. Nature 455, 720–723.

Wuchty, S., Jones, B.F., Uzzi, B., 2007. The increasing dominance of teams in production of knowledge. Science 316, 1036–1039.

SOFT SKILLS AND SELF DECEPTION

Arbinger Institute, 2006. The Anatomy of Peace: Resolving the Heart of Conflict. Berrett-Koehler, San Francisco.

Arbinger Institute, 2010. Leadership and Self-deception: Getting out of the Box. Berrett-Koehler, San Francisco.

Clifton, D.O., Nelson, P., 1992. Soar with your Strengths. Delacorte, New York, NY.

Klaus, P., Rohman, J.M., Hamaker, M., 2007. The Hard Truth about Soft Skills: Workplace Lessons Smart People Wish They'd Learned Sooner. Collins, New York, NY.

SYNCHRONICITY

Cederquist, J., 2009. Meaningful Coincidence: Remarkable True Stories of Synchronicity and the Search for Answers. Marshall Cavendish, London.

Hunt, V.V., 1996. Infinite Mind: Science of the Human Vibrations of Consciousness. Malibu Publishing Co., California.

Jung, C.G., 1965. Memories, Dreams, Reflections. Random House, New York, NY.

Jung, C.G., 2006. Synchronicity: An Acausal Connecting Principle. Routledge, New York.

Kaku, M., Trainer, J., 1987. Beyond Einstein: The Cosmic Quest for the Theory of the Universe. Bantam, Toronto.

Kuhn, T.S., Hacking, I., 2012. The Structure of Scientific Revolutions. University of Chicago, Chicago.

Novak, M., 1976. The Joy of Sports. Basic Books, New York.

Sheldrake, R., 2004. The Sense of Being Stared At and Other Aspects of the Extended Mind. Arrow Books, London.

Strogatz, S.H., 2003. Sync: The Emerging Science of Spontaneous Order. Hyperion, New York.

Wheatley, M.J., 2006. Leadership and the New Science: Discovering Order in a Chaotic World. Berrett-Koehler, San Francisco.

INDEX

Note: Page numbers followed by "*f*" and "*t*" refer to figures and tables respectively.

Printed and bound by CPI Group (UK) Ltd, Croydon, CR0 4YY

08/06/2025

01896868-0005